Years of Grace and Grit

Aerial view of Kehl farm

Also by D. G. Kehl:

The Literary Style of the Old Bible and the New. Indianapolis: Bobbs-Merrill Company, Inc. 1970.

Poetry and the Visual Arts. Belmont, CA.: Wadsworth Publishing Company, 1975.

Control Yourself: Practicing the Art of Self-Discipline. Grand Rapids, MI: Zondervan, 1982.

Years of Grace and Grit:

Growing Up on an Illinois Farm

Del Kehl

Order this book online at www.trafford.com
or email orders@trafford.com

Most Trafford titles are also available at major online book retailers.

Printed in the United States of America.

ISBN: 978-1-4269-1963-3

*Our mission is to efficiently provide the world's finest, most comprehensive book publishing
service, enabling every author to experience success. To find out how to publish your book,
your way, and have it available worldwide, visit us online at www.trafford.com*

Trafford rev. 8/12/2010

 www.trafford.com

North America & international
toll-free: 1 888 232 4444 (USA & Canada)
phone: 250 383 6864 ♦ fax: 812 355 4082

Dedicated:

to the memory of our parents,
Anna and Harry Kehl,
with thankfulness for their legacy,
to the memory of our beloved brothers,
John and Maynard,
whose exemplary lives enriched us all,
to this entire birth family,
with whom we share an eternal bond of kinship,
and to the succeeding generations
of our children and grandchildren
to whom we bequeath our own legacy of grace.

Written by Del Kehl, in collaboration with Mary, Maynard, and Barbara (Kampas), with contributions from Mel and Carolyn. Special thanks also to Kevin and Kenyon for technical assistance and to Wanda for her encouragement.

Introduction: It Takes a Family

"The lines have fallen to me in pleasant places;
indeed, my heritage is beautiful." (Psalm 16:6)

"Blessings are on the head of the righteous … ,
The memory of the righteous is blessed, but the
name of the wicked will rot." (Proverbs 10:6-7)

"How confusing the beams from memory's lamp are;
One day a bachelor, the next a grampa.
What is the secret of the trick?
How did I get so old so quick?"
    (Ogden Nash, *You Can't Get There from Here*)

"No memory of having starred
Atones for later disregard
Or keeps the end from being hard."
    (Robert Frost, "Provide, Provide")

"To the memory nothing is ever really lost."
    (Eudora Welty, *One Writer's Beginnings*)

"These are begot in the ventricle of memory,
nourished in the womb of pia mater,
and delivered upon the mellowing of occasion."
    (Shakespeare, *Love's Labour's Lost*)

It's difficult to know what to call this document because it seems to defy most labels while inviting others. In one sense, it's a personal family history because some genealogical research, checking of dates, and verifying facts were done. It's not a family autobiography, which covers a greater, more comprehensive span, whereas this document attempts to capture certain highlights or meaningful moments in our family's past. "Memoir" would seem to fit best, in that it's a report or record of memorable events compiled by those having intimate knowledge of them and based on personal participation and observation. At times it's anecdotal and objective, but at other times it's inward and subjective. It's more about what can be gleaned from segments of our family's span than about the outcome of the family life as a whole. In a sense, it's a kind of legacy writing, contemplating the meaning of events in retrospect, with particular emphasis on the legacy, especially the spiritual one, left by our forebears. It's a narrative of how some of us remember our lives growing up as a family on an Illinois farm, especially during the difficult days of the Great Depression. We do well to remember the words of the English novelist Anthony Powell: "Memoirs can never be wholly true, since they cannot include every conceivable circumstance of what happened." Furthermore, this one cannot be wholly true because each of us remembers some of the same events differently, subjectively, from different perspectives and different contexts. All who've been a part of this project have been as accurate as our flawed memories permit, but if anyone recalls things differently, we readily concede fallibility. We admit, with the Queen in Lewis Carroll's *Alice in Wonderland*, "It's a poor sort of memory that only works backward," but we also echo Ira Gershwin's words: "The memory of all that—No, no! They can't take that away from me!"

This project began with special encouragement from Barb Kampas, along with the urging of Mary, who did the genealogy research, to record our family story for posterity. Early on we considered such questions as these: Have you ever wondered about why God put each of us in this particular family and in this particular place? How do you think growing up in this place, in this family, affected each of us—our personalities, our characters, our proclivities, our strengths and weaknesses? What traumas and psychological scars, if any, did each of us sustain? What do each of us most treasure and value about the life we lived together? What regrets, if any, does each of us have? What might we each change, if we could go back? And, especially, what specific examples can we see of the sovereign hand of God working through His abundant grace in our lives, protecting, leading, guiding?

In May, 2004, the six Kehl siblings sat around a table in the kitchen at the family farm, flanked by wives and members of their families, and spent about three hours reminiscing, sharing, and recording stories about our memories of growing up together on the farm, one of the few times all six of us sat and remembered together. It's especially poignant in retrospect, because little did any of us know that it would be the last time all six of us would be together before John's home-going six months later. (See Chapter IV for a transcription of this special dialogue.)

One key, recurring idea in that dialogue and in this memoir is praise to our Sovereign Lord for His abundant grace in sparing all of us from close brushes with death, in working through Mother (and a Christian radio program) to lead us to saving faith in Christ, in helping our parents somehow, against great odds, to hang onto the farm through the difficult days of the Great Depression, in leading us to a Bible-believing church, in helping us grow in the Christian life, in enabling us to receive a semblance of a very elementary education in a one-room country school, in propelling us beyond the provincial shyness and traumatic inferiority to fruitful, productive lives.

God had a sovereign purpose for all of these events, both the positive and the negative ones. Though we certainly don't claim to understand it all—or even very much of it—, for we only know "in part," we can recognize better in retrospect the loving, graceful leading of our God. If anyone can read this document and come away failing to see a family "graced," a family living by grit and "grace under pressure" (to use Hemingway's famous definition of "guts"), then the central purpose and underlying idea will be missed. As the American writer George Santayana said, "Religion [we would prefer to say the Christian faith] in its humility restores man to his only dignity, the courage to live by grace." Any dignity, any courage, shown by this family is itself all of grace, a gift of grace from God. This grace (*charis*) is not only "unmerited favor" but ***favor against merit*** (for not only do we not deserve His mercy and lovingkindness but we deserve the very opposite, eternal condemnation); it is that special ability to transform unpleasant or potentially unpleasant circumstances into pleasing ones. This narrative cites numerous examples of this transformation in our lives: for evidence, read on.

A key question underlying this consideration of our family history is: What effect did the family as a whole have on the development of each individual member? This question will be addressed in subsequent chapters. Dr. Norman Wakefield has specified eight things that a family accomplishes. First, the family lays the foundation for the adult personality. Our personalities were formed by both nature (our heredity, our genes) and nurture (our family environment, our upbringing, our interaction with parents and siblings). Chapter III, "The Kehl Siblings: We Are Six," discusses this influence, including birth order. Second, the family creates a mirroring environment in which self-esteem emerges. Or, in some cases, the home environment may foster struggles with self-esteem, producing deep-seated feelings of inferiority. Third, the family shapes the individual's view of and relationship with God, a most significant influence. Chapter VIII, "A Legacy of Faith," discusses how Mother especially was used in this key influence. Fourth, the family influences one's feeling of competency, vocational/educational direction, and life purpose. This influence can be seen in Chapter VI, "Telling Tales Out of School" and several others as well. Fifth, the family creates the context for developing interpersonal skills. We all learned, necessarily, how to get along equitably with each other as well as with extended family, with friends and neighbors, to give and take, to stand up for what is right and also to stand down, sometimes to compromise, other times to challenge and contest. Sixth, the family shapes one's values and character orientation. As noted throughout, but especially in Chapter VIII and Chapter II, our values and character development were modeled by example, action, and behavior in addition to being taught by word of mouth. Seventh, the family serves as a role model for the individual's own marriage and family life. Numerous studies have shown the significant influence of parent/child relations and offspring/spouse relations. Finally, the family serves as the womb of intellectual and emotional stimulation and development. Again, Chapters III and VI touch on this influence. Ours has been "a wonderful heritage" (Psalm 16:6) indeed, for which we are thankful!

In one of his essays, English writer Jerome K. Jerome imagines returning as an adult to meet and converse with himself as a young boy, thinking what he would say and what advice he would offer to his young self. Or imagine what you would say in a letter written to yourself at key stages of growing up—yourself at age 6 beginning 1st grade, at age 13 graduating from 8th grade, at age 17 graduating from high school—and what might your younger self say to you? Such an exercise is, of course, very personal and private, not to be shared in such a document as this, but at least one bit of advice to each of our younger selves might appropriately be something like this: "Look kid, there's no reason in the world for you to feel inferior! You have a lot on the ball, so assert yourself and stop feeling shy, retiring, and lacking in self-esteem. You have immense value because you've been made in the image of God, enabling you in some degree to reflect His attributes; He sent His Son to die for you to redeem you from sin and sent His Holy Spirit to indwell you and guide you; He has a wonderful purpose for your life and has given you special gifts and abilities, having created you to be creative; and He has given you a wonderful, loving family. Thank Him for that. Now go tell Mom and Dad, brothers and sisters, how much you love them!"

The compiling, the writing, and maybe even the reading of this memoir has potential therapeutic value, enabling us to come to terms with some of the traumas of the past as well as resounding to the praise and glory of our Heavenly Father for His abundant grace through the years.

Table of Contents

I. Sense of Place

"… The sense of the place, the savor of the genie-soul of
the place which every place has or else is not a place…
There it is as big as life, the genie-soul of the place
which, wherever you go, you must meet and master first
thing or be met and mastered…. This Midwestern sky is
the nakedest, loneliest sky in America."

(Walker Percy, *The Moviegoer*)

"The end of all our exploring
Will be to arrive where we started
And know the place for the first time."

(T. S. Eliot, "Little Gidding," *The Four Quartets*)

The Region

The Kehl place is located in the gently rolling hills of northwestern Illinois. It's situated in a region shaped roughly like a crescent or triangle (sometimes called the I-88 Corridor), bounded on the east and south by the Rock River, on the west by the Mississippi River and Iowa, on the north by Wisconsin. This region, punctuated in its northeast corner by Rockford and Beloit, its southwest tip by the Quad Cities (Rock Island, Moline, Bettendorf, Davenport), and its northwest tip by East Dubuque and Galena, is arguably one of the most historic and picturesque in the state. It boasts the homes of two U.S. presidents—Grant's home in historic Galena and Reagan's boyhood home in Dixon—as well as other historic places, such as the site of the second Lincoln-Douglas debate in Freeport, the Arsenal Prison for Confederate soldiers at Rock Island, site of the Second Battle of Black Hawk near Kent (a 56-acre battlefield where 23 were ambushed in 1832 and where Abe Lincoln, with militia from Dixon, came to help bury the dead). It includes the scenic 2550-acre Mississippi Palisades State Park north of Savanna, five other state parks, the highest point in Illinois (1,236 feet, near Scales Mound), and other attractions. It encompasses three counties (Carroll, Jo Daviess, Stephenson) and parts of four others (Winnebago, Ogle, Lee, Whiteside). Besides the mighty Mississippi River and Rock River, waterways include the Apple, Galena, Pecatonica, Sugar, and Plum rivers, along with Apple Canyon Lake, Lake Le-Aqua-Na, Spring Lake, and Lake Carroll (manmade). Towns with female names seem to abound in this region—for example, Elizabeth, Lena, Nora, Florence, Pearl City, Adeline, Shannon, Coleta. It was a wonderful place in which to grow up, but as Fred Allen said, "California's a wonderful place to live—if you happen to be an orange," so some might say that northwestern Illinois is a wonderful place to live—if you happen to be a stalk of corn. The Carroll County area itself is said to have been called "Man-I-Tumi" by the Indians, meaning "Land of God."

The Town

The Kehl hometown, of course, is Mount Carroll, named after Charles Carroll of Maryland, the last survivor among the signers of the Declaration of Independence. (Shortly before his death at 95 in 1832, Carroll wrote: "On the mercy of my redeemer I rely for salvation, and on his merits, not on the works I have done in obedience to his precepts.") "Mount" signifies its consideration as a quaint little "city" set on a hill (originally called "Baby Mountain"). The town dates from 1841, when a flour mill was built on Waukarusa Creek (the mill terminated in the 1920s), plotted in 1843 and designated the county seat, but it developed slowly until 1862 with the arrival of the Chicago, Minneapolis, and St. Paul Railroad. Residents reportedly called the town "a bit of New England in the Middle West." In his book *Off the Beaten Path: A Guide to Unique Places*, Bob Puhala devotes 35 pages to Northwestern Illinois, describing Mt. Carroll as "pure nineteenth-century Midwest America with its cobblestone courthouse square in the center of town, Victorian architecture, and 1870's-style storefronts lining Main Street." Another writer has referred to the town's Federal, Italianate, and Queen Anne styles. A 19th century writer described the town and its environs as follows: "The Indians were numerous and friendly. Game and fish were abundant, and so were mosquitoes, flies, and raccoons, also blackbirds, crows, and other birds of prey. In fact, the first corn fields had to be guarded from the depredations of the latter." According to the 2000 census, there were 1,832 residents but 1,704 in 2005, with 41% reporting German ancestry.

Notable features include the town square with its red brick Italianate courthouse, constructed in 1858, and the 1891 Civil War monument, crowned by a cavalryman holding a flag and facing cemetery hill, another facing south and holding a rifle, left leg thrust forward and symbolizing "Endurance," a mustachioed third soldier facing north, his right hand resting on a revolver in his belt and symbolizing "courage." The inscription reads: "Slavery abolished. Carroll County to the memory of the men who saved the Union that their Example may speak to Coming Generations." An annex (1895) of additional names (listed in *Ripley's Believe It or Not* as the only memorial with an annex) is adjacent, along with cannons and bandstand. To the north is the Glen View Hotel, built in 1886. The female "Seminary," which opened in 1853 and later became Shimer College (its Georgian Revival buildings dating from 1905) closed in 1978 and was converted to the Campbell Center for Historic Preservation Studies. *The Christian Science Monitor* described the town as follows: "A small round-paned window here, a few pillars there, a curlicued pediment somewhere else ... (here) is a beautiful town."

Mt. Carroll, Market Street

Courthouse, Mt. Carroll

Civil War monument, Mt. Carroll

We Kehl kids didn't think of the town as especially "beautiful," but I remember the "thrill" of going to town sporadically to attend Sunday School and church at the Methodist Church and, during bad weather and planting and harvest seasons less often, on Saturday afternoon to get groceries at the A & P ("Gonna go down to the A & Pee") or, less often, at Nobles (Red and White) (seldom at Royal Blue), and to stand or sit around to watch who drove repeatedly down Market Street, made a U-Turn at Ivy's Monuments, and back up. Sometimes midweek trips to town were required to get a part for machinery or to get a broken part fixed (I loved to ride with John on his motorcycle on these trips). In town, Dad would sometimes give one of us money to get candy at Marth's ("Now don't get candy with nuts, because you know I can't chew it!") or over-ripe bananas at Nobles. (I recall one time being chided for getting chocolate-covered peanuts, having forgotten that he couldn't eat it.) Less commonly, we might go to Isenharts for a dish of ice cream (Meadow Gold, of course) or a Cherry Coke or a malt. On those trips to town we always hoped (but dared not presume to ask) to stop at Colehours gas station on the way home, for a bottle of Orange or Grape pop!

Major establishments in town included Krafts Clothing Store (on the Kinney Block), Marths Five-and-Dime, *The Mirror Democrat* newspaper office, Carroll Café, Fred Lee's Insurance Office—all on Main Street; Gambles, Coast-to-Coast, Isenhart's Restaurant, Poffenburger's Tavern, Sievert's Tavern, Fay Christian Funeral Home, Ivy's Monuments, Zink's Barber Shop (under the First National Bank)—all on Market Street; the Post Office, Noble's jewelry store, offices of Drs. Mershon and Petty, Franks Furniture and Funeral Home—all on Clay Street.

For me, the most distinctive establishment was the Mt. Carroll Township Public Library on the southwest corner of Main and Rapp Streets, funded by philanthropist Andrew Carnegie in 1907. (Reportedly, Carnegie was so pleased that the two-story brick and stone structure could be built for the $10,000 he had contributed, he donated an additional $10,000 to purchase tables, chairs, and book stacks.) The library, with 1,250 books, opened to the public in August of 1908. (I remember Roberta Williamson, who was librarian from 1928-1959, and Mrs. Seitner shushing for silence and making sure no one presumed to check out more than five books at a time. I spent many hours browsing in the stacks and exploring the less-frequented upstairs rooms.)

Carnegie Library, Mt. Carroll

Adjacent to the library was the Carroll Theatre, but we weren't permitted to attend movies, except for one we attended with Mel—"God Is My Co-Pilot," starring Dennis Day, the title apparently convincing our folks that maybe it wouldn't be too corrupting. Later we saw Gene Autry and Roy Rogers movies, and Dad enjoyed seeing "The Royal Canadian Mounted Police." Farther down Main Street, past the Community House, was the brick grade school and high school (see more in Chapter VI). The town's churches were clustered in this vicinity—Methodist Episcopal (which we attended as children), First Baptist, Evangelical Lutheran, Church of God (directly across from the school), a small Catholic church on a side street, and the Center Hill United Brethren Church a few miles west of town (see more in Chapter VIII).

Methodist Church, Mt. Carroll

Church of God, Mt. Carroll

This little country town is situated not just on one hill but on several, including Punkin Hill on the east side. We moved from the farm to 210 Jackson Street in November of 1952. Mother and Dad did a lot of remodeling—closing up some windows and doors, later digging a septic tank and adding a bathroom designed and planned by Mother. She also drew up the decorative trim for the shelves, and Dad cut them out. Neighbors included Cora Rogers on one side and Mrs. Getz on the other, the McCrays, Cooney Hearse (later Ralph and Mildred Rogers), and the Davises across the street.

House on 210 Jackson Street, Mt. Carroll

The Caroline Mark home, with its well-manicured lawn and nature trails for visitors, is on the northeast side, having been built in 1906 for elderly ladies at no cost to them. Good Samaritan Nursing Home, where Dad resided for several years until his death, is on the northwest edge of town. Point Rock Park, with Castle Rock on Waukarusa Creek, lies below Oak Hill Cemetery, which has gravestones dating back to the 1800s, the inevitable destination of most who remain in Mt. Carroll.

As for other little towns surrounding Mt. Carroll, each of us associates them with particular events and visits. Savanna, for years possessing the only stoplight in Carroll County, boasted a hospital and ordnance depot (referred to as "The Proving Ground"). As both a river and railroad town, Savanna had a certain reputation for wildness (where guys cruised the streets looking for girls). Stockton, north on route 78, was more sedate, where Uncle Chris and Aunt Ida lived and where Chris had his egg/poultry business, where a quaint elevated wooden bridge carried traffic over the railroad yard. I remember Thomson mainly for its melons, both Chadwick and Shannon for visits (cold winter rides in the Model A) to the dentist (Dr. H. H. Hoy, who ironically tried to bribe us into submissive behavior with candy and gum), Milledgeville as the site of the Carroll County Fair (and where Mary worked in the Cheese Factory, slicing and weighing the Swiss cheese), Morrison for the Whiteside Country Fair and the Lincoln Highway that runs through the town, Lanark for the Green Giant Canning Factory (where I worked one summer), Loran and Pearl City mainly as way-points to Freeport, little Massbach as Mother's territory, Warren as site of the Jo Daviess Country Fair, Woodbine as the little town to which Mary and I remember riding with Mother and Dad to make farm loan payments to the Heidenreichs, or later as stop-overs on the way to or from Galena (the latter being my choice of the town with the most charm in the region).

Neighbors and The Neighborhood

The Kehl place is a 249.7-acre farm seven miles north of town, in Carroll County (near the Jo Daviess County line), Freedom Township. Growing up, I recall going to and from town most often by way of "the cement," Highway 78—out the gravel road (for long just rutted mud, sifting dust, or drifting snow), past Judases, Sage School, Tiptons, the Charley Wolf place, left on the highway, past the Billy/Howard Schmidt farm, the Guentzler place, the Kecklers, up Sisler Hill, past the Elizabeth Road and Woodland Road, past Colehour's little gas station at the edge of town, up the hill and over the bridge, past the Glen View Hotel and courthouse square, with the post office on the left. Later, when Meyers Road was blacktopped, it was more common to take that route—down the hill past Nowaks, past the Skunk Hollow turnoff, over Plum River, past the Miseks and Butts places, past the Meyers farms, over the curvy highway (where John's car slid on the ice one winter when he was taking Mary and me to high school), past the Caroline Mark home and the American Legion Hall, onto Route 78 near the bridge.

Surely any history of the Kehl farm and family would be incomplete without some consideration of the two dozen or so neighboring farms and families, which, though isolated in varying degrees, constituted at least a semblance of community. When a shyster lawyer, seeking to justify himself, asked Jesus, "And who is my neighbor?" Jesus related the parable of the Good Samaritan (Luke 10:29), illustrating that a neighbor is a fellow human being, especially one in need, who is nearby (the word itself derived from the Old English *neahgebur*, literally "a nigh farmer"). "A bad neighbor is a misfortune," the 8th century B.C. poet Hesiod said, "as much as a good one is a blessing." The Kehl family was fortunate to have many of the latter and few of the former.

Each of us could make our own list of each kind, probably using some different criteria. Someone has defined a neighbor as "a person who knows more about your affairs than you do." Would a good neighbor be someone who minds his/her own business and lets you mind yours? That seems to be what Marcus Aurelius meant when he said, "How much time he gains who does not look to see what his neighbor says or does or thinks, but only at what he does himself, to make it just and holy." The Roman poet Horace said, "It is your concern when your neighbor's wall is on fire," maybe not because of concern for the neighbor's loss, we might add, but concern for the security of *your own*. Another poet, Robert Frost in "Mending Wall," said, "Something there is that doesn't love a wall, / That wants it down," but his neighbor insists, "Good fences make good neighbors." Most farmers, certainly including Dad and my brothers, would endorse the second view, especially after walking the fence lines following a spring flood, having to repair a neighbor's fence, or driving his cows from our hayfield or cornfield. The Scriptures command us repeatedly to "love your neighbor as yourself" (Leviticus 19:18, Matthew 19:19b, 22:39, Romans 13:9b, Galatians 5:14, James 2:8). English poet George Herbert summed up the matter when he said, "Love your neighbor, yet pull not down your hedge."

It might be helpful to envision the Kehl place as a hub with the neighboring farms in a series of three concentric circles connected by spokes to the center. The first circle, in closest proximity to the center, includes ten neighboring farms and families--the Judases, Tiptons, Nobles/Nowaks, Kaufmans, Boens, Kantlehners, Fredericks, Schmidts, Maders, Beckenkellers/Dixons. The second circle includes eight—Rob Tipton/Charlie Wolf, Randeckers/Deweys, Roy Schuberts, Prestons, Weeks, Wuebbens, Miseks, Lutts. The third circle includes seven—Dindermans, Rausches, Butts, Pollards, Wilsons, Meyers, Howard Schmidts. Some were tenant farmers, struggling to make ends meet and support their families, often a difficult matter if weather—drought, flooding, tornadoes—ruined crops or caused a poor yield, if equipment and feed costs rose and prices for milk, eggs, cattle, and hogs dropped, or if bad management or illness delayed getting the crops in on time, cultivating them, or harvesting them in a timely manner.

Often the demands of constant toil must have seemed oppressive—chores to do in morning and evening, long days working in the fields, often with torrid heat and humidity in summer and bitter, frigid cold and snow or ice in winter. Hamlin Garland's short story "Among the Corn-Rows," set in Iowa, refers to this "bondage to labor." Other writers have referred to still other rigors of farm life during the 30's, 40's, and 50's. In an essay published in 1949, Carson McCullers referred to loneliness as "the great American malady," "aloneness" being "an involuntary and fearful thing ... The sense of moral isolation is intolerable to us." Contributing to the moral and social isolation was the physical isolation of many farms in those days, some accessible only by dirt roads, some of which were hardly more than cow-lanes with grass and weeds growing between the wheel tracks. A few of the farmhouses in circles two and three were accessible only through a "gap" (not even a gate, but barbed-wires nailed on supporting sticks) which had to be opened, then closed to keep livestock confined—or maybe strangers out. Driving through backcountry roads often presented a vista of isolation and desolation, with farmhouses crouching stark amid outbuildings, all sometimes badly in need of repair and paint. Isolation was even greater during the years when we had no electricity, no television, no telephone, though we did receive a newspaper (*The Clinton Herald*) which arrived a day late by mail (which, during muddy or snowy times sometimes required a mile walk to the "pavement" of route 78), but thankfully, we did have a little Philco radio to provide some news from the outside world and to bring the Good News of God's grace to our family.

Each farmhouse harbored its own story, many of them sad. How many an Ethan Frome (the farmer ruined physically and psychologically in Edith Wharton's novella of that title) was hidden away in isolation? All three circles included their share of diverse, rather eccentric, even grotesque figures who could have come from Sherwood Anderson's novel *Winesburg, Ohio,* but as Anderson wrote in "The Book of the Grotesque," "The grotesques were not all horrible. Some were amusing, some almost beautiful," like the gnarled, twisted apples left by the pickers but which are deliciously sweet. For example, there was the former United Brethren preacher who lived by himself in a ramshackle house, the junk dealer who lived in a small house surrounded by rusting cars, three brothers who lived by themselves in their decaying family homestead, an immigrant farmer referred to as "the Old Bohemian," a Chicago man who bought a local farm and rented the fields but let the buildings fall into ruin, a celibate farmer who lived with his mother and sister, a country preacher whose hellion son was often seen coming home from his night out when farmers were going to the fields, the farmer who loved to tell about how it was done "out in Nebrasky where I was at," a tenant farmer with eight kids who drank away much of his profit on Saturday night binges. Other stories were tragically violent—for example, the farmer who was killed during haymaking when the gigantic poles used for stacking hay collapsed and struck him or the farmer's wife who was killed when the power take-off shaft on the tractor came loose and struck her head.

Most farm families were honest, hard-working, and stoical. Some were "neighborly," working together during "haying" (before hay-balers were common) and "threshing" (before "combines" replaced threshing machines), sometimes corn-picking (before the advent of mechanical corn-pickers), whereas some kept to themselves and worked alone. On at least one occasion, when a farmer was disabled, neighbors came in and harvested his crops for him. Dad and my brothers modeled good neighborliness, often helping neighboring farmers with crops, fixing broken machines or cars, and butchering—often receiving no remuneration of any kind.

Threshing began when the oats, barley, wheat, or rye ripened, in late July and August, running for several months. The men were usually gone from home from July to corn-picking time. Initially, Grandpa Mike and John Randecker worked as partners with a wooden threshing machine run by horse power—usually six or eight horses walking in a circle, with the driver sitting on a platform in the middle of the circle, the gears and shaft running out from the middle to the threshing machine. Dad was just a young kid when he drove the horses. Later Grandpa Mike and John Randecker purchased a steel threshing machine, but the horses couldn't power it, working up a sweat in just a short time, so the partnership ended, with Randecker taking the old machine and Grandpa the new one. Then Grandpa bought a Case steam engine at Squires Hardware store in Mt. Carroll, having to wait for it to be delivered by train. The engine burned coal, which the host farm supplied. Because few farmers in the area had a steam engine and threshing machine, word soon spread, and Grandpa, Dad, and hired man John Reed (who hauled the water) threshed for surrounding area farms in Jo Daviess and Carroll Counties, as far east as the current day Lake Carroll (near Lanark). (According to one story, the hired man, who stayed at the farm while the boys were small, was too lazy to get up at night and go outside to urinate, so he peed out the window—until Mother nailed the window shut.)

Threshing crew

Steam engine

Initially, the threshing crew would stack the grain in large stacks and then pull the machine up close to the stack and pitch the grain into the machine. A few years later, farmers began to put the grain in bundles and shocks. The binder tied the bundles with twine, dropped them in the bundle carrier, and, when the bundle carrier was full, it would be tripped. Then the men would stand eight bundles on end, with one spread on top. When it was time to thresh, the shocks were pitched up on the wagon with a pitchfork, hauled to the threshing machine, and pitched into the machine. Occasionally the binder would miss tying a bundle, and it would need to be tied by hand if the twine could be found; if not, Dad was an expert at making a "band" out of oat stalks to tie the bundle. Ordinarily, there were seven wagons hauling bundles, with three or four men to pitch.

The "ring" crew would stay at the farm where they were threshing until the job was completed. The women would work together and prepare a sumptuous meal for the crew, with the men being served first and the women and children eating later. (See Chapter VII for more on food.) Sometimes at bedtime, the house would be locked and workers would have to sleep in the barn; in some cases, the barn wasn't so bad because some of the homes were not so nice, having bedbugs and other unwelcome features.

When Dad took over the farm, he continued the threshing ring. At each farm, Dad assigned jobs to the farmers and oversaw the operation. He had three wagons to haul bundles. (Maynard, John, and Charles Havorka pitched bundles for him. George Lutts, Frank Havorka, Ritchie Beckenkeller, and Roy Kaufman hauled bundles, with Oscar Rausch and Harry Dinderman shoveling oats.) One year while the crew was threshing at the Kaufman farm, Maynard pitched nine big loads of bundles in a single day. As soon as one load was pitched, there would be another wagon waiting to be done. On the other hand, when a neighbor had his threshing ring, it took him three or four days to complete the job whereas Dad would do it in one day. Maynard and John pitched for this ring, but would have time to run down to the river to skinny-dip between wagon loads. When they heard the wagon coming, they'd scurry out of the water, dress, and hop on the back of the wagon to pitch another load.

During the threshing season of 1941, the crew were moving the machinery to the Dinderman farm to thresh. They had to cross Plum River at the Rausch farm. Mel, who was driving the Titan, had trouble driving it out the other side because of the steep crossing. John, just 13 years old, tried to back the Fordson tractor down to pull the Titan out, but having no brakes, the Fordson started rolling down into the river. Mel was really scared as he saw the tractor rolling down the crossing, thinking he was going to lose both his dad and his brother, but Dad ran alongside, grabbed the steering wheel, and cramped it enough to get it stopped—yet another evidence of God's sovereign, gracious protection.

One Monday morning, after the crew had threshed a little, Charlie Kruse, who worked for Dad and who loved to run around at night, was sleeping behind the straw stack. The Noble boys, who loved to aggravate, put Mel up to pouring water on Charlie, so Mel climbed up on top of the straw pile and poured water on the sleeping Charlie. Of course, that made Charlie mad and he began to run around the straw pile yelling, "I'm gonna 'nik nor nass" (he had a speech impediment), but he ran into Dad, who promptly told him, "If anybody's gonna' kick anybody's a--, it'll be me." That simmered Charlie down right away.

Grandpa Mike always raised Timothy grass for the cows, but Dad found out quickly that Timothy grass didn't make very good feed, so he chose to raise clover. If he got it made by the 4th of July and then got a good rain, it would come back and make excellent seed. He'd hull the second crop and sell it, making more from the clover seed than from the corn. Dad and Dan Randecker bought a rock crusher and crushed limestone to spread on their fields, then planted alfalfa for hay and made three crops of clover.

There was very little socializing among farm neighbors, except for school "socials," programs, and picnics or occasional shivarees and the ice-cream suppers that followed. One time Mother invited neighbors to a special coon-roast with all the trimmings. (I recall going, as a little kid, with my brother John, driving the old Model-T, to Lew Sites' farm, where he was to fix Lew's old car, which he did but refused any payment; while he was working, Mrs. S. took me into her warm kitchen and gave me coconut macaroons and a glass of milk. After all those years, I still remember those delicious macaroons and her act of kindness to a little kid.) Another neighborhood "social" event of sorts was the morning a yellow Piper Cub airplane landed in a neighbor's pasture, and Dad took us kids down for rides. Only later did we learn that pilot Ridenour earned notoriety for flying upside down, doing loop-de-loops, and swooping under bridges.

The Kehl boys were good friends with various neighbor boys— especially the Fredericks, who sometimes came over on Sunday afternoons, but also the Tiptons, Randeckers, and Judases. They and the Fredericks enjoyed swimming and playing in Plum River to cool off after working in the fields or threshing. This was also their weekday "bath tub." Floyd Frederick was older and looked out for all the boys. The Randecker kids (Mabel, Alice, Wilma, and Danny aka "Fiddlepants"), who lived on the farm on "Dewey Hill," were also good friends. Maynard remembers that Bob Mader lost his wallet in the pigpen. Of course, the pigs found it, played with it, and shook all the money out. The wind blew the bills all over, and Maynard found a $10 bill under the car. Maynard used to park his motorcycle at Rob Tipton's place (later Charlie Wolf's place) when the road was too muddy to ride home. They allowed him to keep it in their shed until the mud dried up and Maynard could walk back to get it.

It was said that Frank Butts thought John should marry one of his daughters. Arta Lou Frederick was also apparently "interested" in him. (Marian Judas reportedly said, "You have to have a number to go out with Johnnie Kehl." One time Marv Judas and John were out "running around" (the expression used then) and picked up a couple of girls; when they both got in the back seat with John, he told them, "One of you better get up in the front with Marv." Another time, Marv, Carl Ross, and John were riding to Savanna, three on the motorcycle. A policeman stopped them and gave them a citation for having too many on the cycle, so one had to get off and wait by the side of the road until John came back to pick him up.

Still another time, one night when Maynard and John went to town they had car trouble—a bolt "busted" off the battery and blew the headlights out. Charlie Havorka offered to follow them home, but it was hard to see, especially on curves, so Charlie went ahead, but he drove too fast and with snow on the ground, Maynard couldn't see and ran off the road into a ditch. Of course, it was in the middle of the night when they went to get help from Albert (Capp) Zink and woke him up. He had to get his tractor out, put water in it (requiring the starting of a gas engine pump), crank it up and running—no small chore—but he finally got them pulled out and on their way. During the war no one could buy tires. The boys tried to make a bike with corn-plow wheels, but it didn't work. Another time Maynard and John's bike tires had holes in them, so the boys mixed up some patching plaster, poured it in the pump, and pumped it into the tire, but it shot out the holes—another exercise in futility!

The spring following Maynard's 18th birthday, he was sent to Chicago on the train to get his army physical, along with Sherm Frederick and Harold Butts. They were ordered to get in line, and when they were told to "drop their pants" embarrassment ensued—whoops, no undershorts, never had worn any. In another line, Maynard overheard a commotion—Harold Butts arguing with the sergeant, something just never to be done! Needless to say, Harold didn't pass the physical (or was it the psychological?). Maynard was classified 1-A, but the war ended before he was drafted. John was able to get farm deferment status.

The Dindermans lived a couple of "hollers" east of the Kehl farm. Dad used to thresh for Harry Dinderman. The first time Maynard saw Bernice was when her dad came over to the farm to ask about threshing. He brought the two girls (Bernice and Darlene) along, and they played with Carolyn and Mary during the morning while the men talked. Bernice was about eleven, and Maynard was about fifteen. They only saw each other over the next few years during threshing time. When Bernice was sixteen, Maynard began to go to see her. The story goes that John was also interested in "seeing" her, but was set straight one day while in the milking barn. He told John, "You leave her alone; she's mine!" They rode on Maynard's motorcycle or in his "Puddle Jumper," which Maynard and John got, minus an engine, from George Lutz, the United Brethren preacher. So the family wouldn't know where he was going, he'd turn and go up past Maders to fool them when he was heading over to the Dinderman farm. John knew where he was off to, but not Dad. When helping to cut wood at the Rausch farm, Maynard would work hard to get done so he could go see Bernice and have dinner.

The usual evening out was a "picture show" (for 35 cents), then to Isenhart's for a butterscotch or chocolate malt (15 cents), with stop for gas on the way home (cost for the entire evening—$2.00). They also spent time riding motorcycles together. One time they rode to Monroe, Wisconsin, and attended the county fair. Maynard enjoyed going to the Dindermans for Sunday dinner, because Mrs. Dinderman was such a great cook. She would make him special treats, such as chicken and noodles, raisin pie. She liked to have Maynard come and enjoyed joking with him. He would repair her gas washer or take a look at Mr. Dinderman's car or tractor, these "repairs" being an excellent reason to keep going to the Dinderman farm. After two years and wearing out two cars (according to Maynard, but Bernice says they were worn out to begin with), they were married on April 18, 1948.

Most neighbors trusted each other, not locking their houses when they left. What a sense of shock and violation we felt when, returning home from church one Sunday, we discovered that someone had been in our house, but apparently hadn't stolen much except my brother's rare

Indian Head pennies and Buffalo nickels. Thereafter, the doors were always securely locked and a light secured on a pole in the barnyard. Once during the night Dad thought someone was stealing gas from the huge gas tank and another time grapes from the grape arbor. Other negative memories include several times when strangers from Chicago came out and hunted on our property without asking permission. Hearing the shooting back in the "timber," Dad, Maynard, and John, armed with their 12-gauge shotguns and 22-caliber rifles, went back to confront them and order them off the property. Mother, I'm sure, prayed earnestly for their safety, and God graciously answered the prayers, causing those potentially tragic confrontations to be resolved peacefully.

The Farm

Arriving at the farm, from either the north or south, presents a picturesque vista of the big white farmhouse and outbuildings set on the hill, "Mount Kehl." Grandpa Kehl, Michael, bought the farm in March of 1883 (reportedly for $6,202), Dad in March of 1924 (reportedly for $10,000), John in June of 1972, and Mike in January of 1999. The first impression is set by the spacious lawn, always well manicured, well shaded by giant oaks (including the mammoth "Bell Tree" opposite the front door and the "Butcher Tree" farther down (used in suspending cows and pigs for butchering), maples, ashes, and cottonwood trees (including what Mother, with still a hint of German accent, called the "tree-trees" near the drive). Other trees included a pear, an evergreen, a cherry, some elderberry trees in "the ditch," a mulberry tree down in the "hog pasture," and a variety of apple trees in the orchard. The yard had an indentation which marked the course of an old road. North of the house, over the hill, was "Old House Holler" where the original log house, first on the homestead, had existed.

Mother recruited Carolyn, Mary, and me, when we came home from school, to rake leaves in early spring, pile them up, and burn them. (I especially loved to pile damp leaves on the fire and watch the smoke roll, so much so one year that the neighbors drove up to see if the house was on fire!). If it was windy, Mother just led us in raking *with the wind*. When they were around ten or twelve, Maynard and John raked the leaves and put them in the outhouse—and received a spanking from Mother. It was my job to keep the grass mowed, hardly finishing one mowing when it would be time to begin all over again. Mother had long dreamed of having abundant flowers growing around the house, but chickens could scratch them out and farm animals could eat and trample them. Finally, at long last, she got the fence she had requested—just a short time before the move to town. But she did enjoy the petunias she planted in the unique window box Dad made for her from an old Fordson tractor gas tank cut in half, painted green to match the shutters, and hung by chains under the south window of the kitchen.

Also conspicuous were the enormous gardens Mother superintended—in at least five different locations, at different times—across the lane from the house (also the location of the Concord grape arbor), across the road (where, among other things, we had strawberries, ground-cherries, and huckleberries), behind the granary (also the location of the blackberry patch, where I remember Carolyn picking berries—barefoot), down behind the old "Wash House" (a strawberry patch—when Uncle Clyde and Aunt Edna were visiting one spring, Mother yelled, "You kids get out of the strawberry patch; you'll spoil your dinner!" only to learn that Clyde was the main "culprit"), and back in the pasture past the machine shed (where we raised lots of strawberries, watermelons, muskmelons or cantaloupes, and potatoes). (See Chapter VII for more on food.)

The farmhouse itself was something of a marvel (where I figure I spent approximately 5500 days and nights, from 1936 to 1952, when we moved to town), consisting of six rooms upstairs and six downstairs. The stairs had fourteen creaking steps, making it difficult to navigate without detection. Upstairs, at the head of the stairs, was "the big room" where Mother and Dad slept. It had space for several beds and dressers. When the boys were little, they slept in this room also, and at bedtime, they would all lie there asking Dad questions and hearing his answers and stories about threshing, trapping, and animals. (According to Maynard, Dad kept his supply of dynamite under his bed, maybe so the boys wouldn't get into it.) The adjoining north room was named "the Meat Room" because, since there was no heat in that room, sugar-cured hams and other meats were sometimes stored there. It had an attic and chimney (where bees often settled) and a small closet, the only one upstairs (apparently, they stored a lot of clothes in dressers in those days). Next to that room was the "Clothes Room," which functioned primarily as a place to hang clothes, on a long pole or rod that ran the length of the room. Across the hall was a small room which Carolyn and Mary shared, and, in the "addition," down two steps and through a low door ("Watch your head!"), was Mel and Maynard's room when they grew older. When that part of the house was added on, the carpenter put the lock on the wrong side of the door. One morning when Maynard got up, the door was locked and he couldn't get out, so he took his pliers and broke the lock to get out, then later welded it and put it back on so no one knew any different. The far east room, with attic, accessible through a small hole in the ceiling, and stovepipe going through it, was the one John and I shared.

Downstairs were the large kitchen, with a door on the north and one on the south, and, on the east a washroom (with water pail, wash basin, and "slop bucket") and woodbox room (with a wooden box for firewood, space for hanging coats and placing overshoes, along with a trap door to the cellar). Part of the large kitchen was used for dining, the whole area with an oak floor (that required frequent applications of oil). Between the kitchen/dining room and "the Other Room" (family room/living room), as it was called, was a small pantry where crocks of pickles were kept, along with shelves for papers, important documents being kept in "the Social Box." The north room, with doors always kept closed, was cold in winter and relatively cool in summer, with an outside door on the west side and the only carpet in the house. In this room the piano was kept, which Mother sometimes was prevailed upon to play (for example, such songs as "Red Wing," "Battle Hymn of the Republic," "Ole Black Joe," and "Tenting Tonight on the Old Camp Ground"), and an elegant (to us) Morris chair. (Maynard and John also stored their stretched mink and muskrat hides here to dry until they could ship them off.) Next to this room was the "birthing room," where all of the Kehl kids were born, a room hardly big enough for a bed and dresser. Adjacent to this room was a small closet called "the luminzimmer" ("rag closet").

Several years ago when John and Edna were remodeling the kitchen, they found, in the wall, a little girl's gingham hat. No one knows whose it was, how it got in the wall, or how it survived all those years! What stories the house could undoubtedly tell! Also in the wall was a copy of *The Galena Weekly Gazette*, dated Thursday morning, September 7, 1899, price $1.50 per annum in advance. The newspaper records such items as: the account of a baby born in New York, weighing just 1½ pounds, the 51st Iowa Regiment preparing to leave Manila, a harvest home picnic held in Speer's Grove near Hanover on last Thursday, which was a most enjoyable affair, along with further news "Over in Badgerdom."

A large cellar runs the full length of the house, accessible outside on the east and by a trap door off the kitchen. (I recall as a little kid running from the west window to the east window to see Maynard riding his Indian motorcycle down the lane—and tumbling down the cellar stairs because someone had left the trap door open.) Potatoes were kept in a large bin, and "the Arch Cellar," a deeper cellar (reportedly added when Dad was about three) with an arched ceiling and with cool temperatures, even in the heat of summer, served as a kind of underground refrigerator for milk, cream, and butter, along with numerous jars of canned fruits, vegetables and meat, as well as sugar-cured beef, and crocks of sauerkraut.

Steps into arch cellar, Kehl Farmhouse

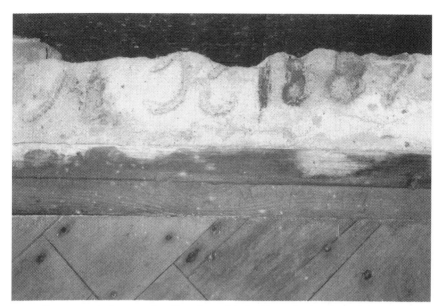

Inscription above arch cellar door: M.K. (Grandpa Mike Kehl) 1887

The cellar also served as a welcome family refuge during tornadoes. The upper cellar is where for some years Mother kept her incubators for hatching chickens, which were then transferred to the "bruder-house." Also, the cellar is where the light-plant, for generating electricity for five to seven years, was located before the REA "high line" came through in 1949. Dad didn't think we needed the REA electricity on the farm; then the war came along, during which time no more lines were installed. Before Maynard wired the house and installed the light-plant, we used kerosene lamps and lanterns.

We all have fond memories of that house, with the old Majestic wood stove for cooking and heating, with its copper reservoir for heating water (carried in from the cistern) for washing and bathing (ordinarily on Saturday nights, in a wooden tub in the cellar). Each of us, at one time or another, sat warming his/her backside on the oven door, drying out mittens on the high-shelf, checking to see if the fire needed more wood (hearing the sizzle when Dad spit tobacco into the stove). Wood was used for cooking and heating. Early on, Dad chopped down the trees and the boys sawed them into workable lengths with a crosscut saw after school (before the purchase of the two-man McCullough chain saw). Sometimes, if they didn't get the wood hauled up to the house, they would have to dig in the snow for it.

In "the Other Room" there was the pot-bellied heating stove, which burned big chunks of wood and, banked at bedtime, radiated heat all night. The stovepipes conveyed some heat upstairs (and the one from the kitchen through the room John and I shared also served as a convenient gong for Dad to rap on with the stove poker to wake us in the morning, if the smell of coffee and buckwheat pancakes didn't get to us first). (Ordinarily, Dad got up first and started the fire in the cook stove before waking Mother to get breakfast.) Frost often coated the windows in winter, but it stayed warm enough for Mother's Christmas cactus to survive all winter long in the "Other Room" by the west window. (I recall sitting with my feet propped up on the railing of the stove, reading for hours while snow and sleet blew against the windows or rain pattered on the tin roof of our upstairs room, or on rainy days crawling up in the attic to go exploring through the boxes of old pictures and other stuff.)

In the earlier years, the family had a telephone, a crank one hung on the wall and, of course, with ten families sharing a "party line." When a call came in, the phone rang in each house, each party having a designated number of rings. Of course, some neighbors "rubbered in" on other calls. When times got hard, during the Depression years, Dad had the phone taken out, some time around 1934, after which, if they needed to make a call, they went to one of the neighbors (as they did when Grandpa Mike died in 1934).

We all had our chores to perform, even as early as six years old. Keeping the woodbox filled with wood, carried from the woodpile, was Maynard's job and later mine. Carrying in the water from the well was Maynard's job and later Mary's, along with gathering the eggs; Carolyn's was feeding the chickens and, when we had goats, milking them. John, Maynard, and Mel all helped with the milking and feeding the cows hay in winter, feeding the pigs ("slopping the hogs") and chickens.

There were fourteen outbuildings, depending on how they are tabulated. One of the most used, of course, was the two-seat outhouse (or privy or "heisley," as Mother called it) (super-cold and drafty in winter, super-hot in summer) south of the house, stocked with a Sears, Roebuck or Montgomery Ward catalogue and with, appropriately, an adjacent lilac bush, which bloomed early in spring. (Mary remembers a new hole being dug for the outhouse when she was four—and was the first to pee in it.) A bit farther south and east was the wash house and just north of the farmhouse was the smoke house and a storage shed (where, for a while at least, the corn planter was stored). Just west of that there was, in the early days, a garage where Dad stored his car and other assorted things. Farther west of that, there was, for a while, a small shed, where John and Maynard kept their motorcycles. Just east of the smokehouse there was a workshop, complete with long workbench and pit for working on cars. The log shop, one of the oldest buildings on the place, consisted of two sections, one for blacksmithing, with forge and anvil, the other section with workbench, lots of tools, and space for storing the Fordson tractor. (According to Maynard, Dad purchased the Fordson new, along with a plow and disk from a dealer in town for $500 or $600.) Maynard installed wind generators, one on each end of the shop.

Farm outbuildings (log shop, granary, corncrib)

Farther north was the bruderhouse, where Mother kept her little chickens (and which was blown over during one tornado, killing all the chicks). The granary had bins for oats and a grinder for grinding oats and corn for feed. An adjoining section on the east served as a garage, where Dad used to store his car. Farther east still was a huge machine shed, consisting of two sections, one where tractors were kept (FarmAll, with steel wheels, used for plowing corn, Allis-Chalmers, Fordson), the other where the threshing machine and clover huller were kept, along with the Old Titan (currently on display at Bechman Mills Park, near Beloit, Wisconsin), steam engine, and when he was away in the Navy, Mel's car.

The corn crib consisted of two parts for storing corn, with space in one for a corn-sheller and, between, space for storing tractors (e.g., the Ford-Ferguson), the Puddle Jumper, etc. and, overhead, the cutter-sleigh. The old log stable had two compartments and a haymow (where cats loved to birth their kittens). The cowshed, farther south and east, provided shelter in winter for cows, where also Dad's 1912 Model-T was stored. The hog house, with two stories, and the chicken house, also with two stories, were adjacent. The 50-foot windmill pumped water from the well (180 feet deep) when there was wind; a hand pump had to be used when there was no wind. (One of the often-recounted family incidents occurred when Mary, just a few years old, was missing at mealtime, then was noticed when Mel looked out the window and saw her halfway up the ladder on the windmill. Dad climbed up to rescue her and the next day, at the insistence of Mother, sawed off the bottom half of the ladder to prevent a repeat of any such recurrence.) Next to the windmill was the horse tank (which provided ice for making ice cream, a task Carolyn and I readily performed, smashing up the ice on the cement slab in front of the corn crib, trading off turning the handle, then taking out the "ribs" and sampling our product before packing it away in a nearby snowdrift for our after-dinner dessert).

The farm land itself consists of ample pastures, woods (or "timber") (including a section of stream called "The Branch"), and, in addition to the garden areas mentioned above, five major fields for raising, in rotation, corn, hay (alfalfa, sometimes clover), and oats. (One year, Dad raised cane in the field across the road, taking it down to the Rausches to be made into sorghum.) Farm animals included beef cows (providing just enough milk for family consumption (except for one year or so when we bought milk and cream from Judases), pigs (the spotted Poland China variety), horses in the early days (I can barely recall the last two, Barney and Roany), lots of chickens (and ducks and geese before my time, but I do recall guinea hens).

There was always a family dog on the farm. "Old Yuck," the first Maynard can remember, was a fox hound/pit bull mix who loved to kill snakes (there were ample bull snakes, garter snakes, and blue racers). Someone would yell "Here Yuck," and he'd come running. All they'd need to do was point at the snake, and Yuck would grab and shake. You had to get back—because the pieces would fly! Yuck lived on ground hogs, killing at least one a day, sometimes two (they didn't buy dog food in those days). The boys helped Yuck catch gophers and ground hogs by drowning them out of their holes. They'd come running out, and the dog would catch them. Sadly, Yuck died mysteriously around 1939; the folks always thought a neighbor shot him. Later they had an English shepherd named Silver. They paid $7.00 for him, and he was sent to the farm from Ohio on the train. A tough old dog, he was once run over by the tractor, lay back in the field several days, then finally came home and recovered from his injuries. Silver would often tree squirrels down in the hollow and wait until one of the boys would go down and shoot them for him. Maynard took Silver with him when he and Bernice got married and moved to the farm out "on the hill," kept him in the barn for several days so he could get adjusted to his new home, but he went back home when they let him out. Silver loved to run around at night, sometimes coming home with shot in him. He lived to age 15. "Sport," a coon hound, lived on the farm at the same time as "Silver." "Butch," brought from California by Mel, was adopted and cared for by Mary and me. According to Mother, he pined away and died of loneliness when I left for college.

There was also the pet pigeon, Mel's pet squirrel (which chewed pencils and other wooden objects in the house), Maynard and John's pet crow (which rode on the axle of a truck to a neighbor's house, then jumped out).

There were always cats hanging around the stable, hoping for milk, supposedly holding down the mice infestation, propagating profusely every year with litters in the haymow (puny or sickly kittens sometimes disposed of in creative but unmentionable ways). Mel, Maynard, and John didn't like cats (and we won't repeat some of the tales regarding them). But according to one story, Mel and Maynard, probably around 8 and 10 years old, made an electric fence charger from a Model-T coil and put it on the window box of the house; when the cats would jump up on the metal window box, they would get "buzzed." When Mother saw what was happening, she scolded them and made them disconnect the charger. They supposedly hooked it up to keep the cats out of the flowers—or was it to watch the cats get "juiced"? (They also tried tying their tails together and stringing them over the clothesline and putting turpentine on their posteriors and watching them run.)

One field and section of timber (where the boys built a hunting blind) were across the road; another was across the lane to the north, stretching down to the Old House Hollow; across the Old House Hollow (where there was a limestone crusher) was the field adjoining the Schmidt place; farther to the east was the field adjoining the Kantlehner place, with more timber to the south; the Sink Hole (attempts were made to fill it up with stumps) field was to the east, with pasture running down to more timber (with The Sand Bank) and pasture running to The Branch; and directly south of the house was the hog pasture with huge boulders protruding.

The farm was quite self-sufficient in many ways, with Dad and the boys necessarily being jacks-of-all trades—besides regular hard-working farmers, agronomists, horticulturists, botanists, arborists, lumberjacks, animal husbandmen, veterinarians, hunters, mechanics, blacksmiths, carpenters, and all-around Mr. Fixits.

An interesting (weekly) event was washday. Without electricity, it was necessary to carry the water, heat it on the cook stove in a copper kettle, then dip it out into a pail and put it in the old wooden washing machine. In the summer, Mother, with help from the girls, washed outside. Each load had to be washed fifteen minutes—by hand, then put through a hand ringer into a wooden tub to be rinsed, then in another tub to be rinsed again, then hung on the clotheslines just south of the house. In winter, the clothes froze and had to be brought in and hung up to finish drying. Of course, nothing was "drip dry." All shirts and dresses had to be ironed—with a flat iron heated on the cook stove. Mother also made soap out of lye and cooked it in a huge butcher kettle outside, then cut it into pieces for use in washing clothes and dishes until we moved to town.

It's been said that revisiting, even just in memory, the place where you grew up is like rereading a favorite book you read first in childhood. I suppose the revisit is like the reread mainly because of the memory jogs, one evoking another, which, in turn, evokes yet another, each with its accompanying nostalgia. Of course, only the books remain unchanged (allowing, of course, for ravages of bookworms, mildew, assorted stains and spots, dog-eared pages, and defacing notes), because places invariably change, but then so do we—and how we read all three.

II. Kehl Family History: A Sense of Roots

"God sets the solitary in families .... He makes his families like a flock."   (Psalm 68:6, 107:41)

"My son, observe the commandment of your father,
And do not forsake the teaching of your mother;
Bind them continually on your heart;
Tie them around your neck.
When you walk about, they will guide you;
When you sleep, they will watch over you;
And when you awake, they will talk to you."
                                        (Proverbs 6:20-22)

"Happy families are all alike; every unhappy family is unhappy in its own way."
                              (Leo Tolstoy, *Anna Karenina*)

"The family: a unit composed not only of children, but of men, women, an occasional animal, and the common cold."

                                        (Ogden Nash)

Great-Grandparents, Grandparents

Our great-grandparents on both sides of the family came from Germany, so we clearly have German roots and often, justifiably or not, claim a ready alibi for displaying one of those supposed German traits, such as quick temper, moodiness, stubbornness. Our paternal great-grandfather, Anton Kehl, was born in 1803 in Baden Baden, Germany, came to Pennsylvania in early manhood, then in 1847 moved first to the Galena area, subsequently to Camp Creek, Derinda Township, Jo Daviess County, where (in 1853) he and his (second) wife, Margaretha Fehler, were among the earliest settlers. According to the *Historical Encyclopedia of Illinois and History of Carroll County*, he made a claim on government land, built a cabin, and walked all the way to the land office at Dixon to enter his claim. This historical document states that "he became prosperous because of his energy and industry and at the time of his death [in 1863] was the owner of a fine farm." We can be thankful for and proud of such an illustrious forebear. Grandpa Mike was only about eight when his father Anton died.

Michael William Kehl, our paternal grandfather, was born in 1855 in Jo Daviess County and married Caroline Schubert in 1883. (Could Franz Peter Schubert, the great German composer, have been distant relation?) Grandpa, in the snapshot with his vest and handlebar mustache or the one of him standing next to Dad in their jackets, boots, and cap or hat, bears a striking resemblance to Mark Twain. They had eight children; our father Harry William Kehl, was the second-born in 1886, and his seven sisters were: Ella, Ida, Lula, Cora, Frances, Florence, and Edna. (Look at that early snapshot of them all, with Dad perched on the left, Ella on the right, and Edna as a baby in the center, or note the later one, taken on the farm, with Dad on the far right in his bib-overalls and blue shirt.) Grandpa and Grandma reportedly had their favorites among the Kehl siblings. According to one story, once when Mother spanked Carolyn, Grandpa said the boys should have received it instead.

Grandpa Michael Kehl (Dad's father)

Grandpa Mike with Dad, Harry

Dad Kehl with 7 sisters (early)

Dad Kehl with 7 sisters (later)

Grandpa Mike was mechanically inclined and could repair any piece of machinery, a trait which was passed on to Dad and grandsons Mel,

Maynard, and John. He and John Randecker custom-sawed wood for neighbors, making about $10 a cord. Randecker would file the saw blade, but he didn't do a good job—and ruined it. Grandpa Mike would remove it at the end of the day and take it home to file, showing son Harry how to file it properly. After that Dad became quite proficient at filing and would file it expertly on the job. The other men helping with the job made fun of Randecker because he didn't file the blade correctly, but the "kid" had to do it right. One cold winter day, Randecker was trying to loosen the 3 or 4" nut on the bolt that held the blade on the shaft, swinging the hammer with one hand. Dad cautioned him not to hit it so hard or the shaft would break, but Randecker didn't like it that a kid was telling him what to do, so he took the hammer in both hands and continued to hit the nut—and, sure enough, the shaft broke. What they would have made that day it cost them to have a new shaft made at Kipnis' Machine Shop in town (located in the flats near Waukarusa Creek. (The old shaft was used for years to prop open the farmhouse cellar door.)

Grandpa and Grandma Kehl moved to Punkin Hill in Mt. Carroll. Grandma Caroline reportedly had dementia in her later years, and sometimes wandered away from their home. When she passed away in 1929, Grandpa moved back to the farm, and he lived five years until his death in 1934 at age 79. Mel and Maynard remember Grandpa Mike being laid out in his coffin in the living room and the family, neighbors, and friends sitting up all night with the body, as in a wake.

Our maternal great-grandfather, Johannes Albrecht, was born in 1816 in Alsace, France, married Christina Shelenberger in 1847, emigrated to the US, and settled in the Massbach area. (Note that snapshot of them, seated, both looking sad or just sternly stoic, he looking straight on, she looking off to the right as if disinterested, holding something in her hands. What might she be holding?)

Great Grandparents (Maternal)

Our maternal grandfather was John Albrecht, born in 1861, one of eleven children. (A snapshot shows him to be a strikingly handsome man with full beard and upsweep flash of hair.)

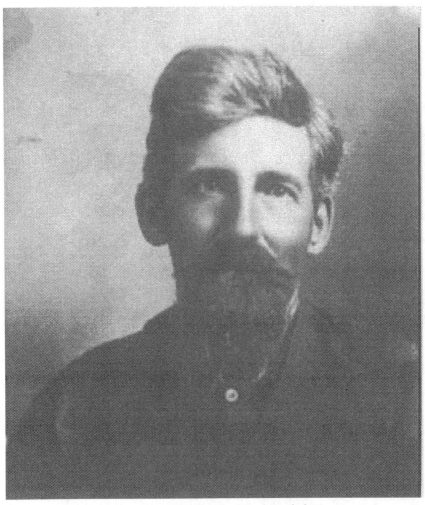

Grandpa John Albrecht (Mother's father)

He married Christiana Randecker, and they had five children: our mother Anna (sometimes printed as Annie, though she signed "Anna") Carrie Albrecht, was the third-born in 1897, and her four brothers were: John, Christopher, Ludwig, and Rudolph.

Anna Kehl with 4 brothers (early)

Anna Kehl with 4 brothers (later)

(How sad it was that Grandpa was to die in 1914 at the relatively early age of 53, of a burst appendix, when Mother was just 17.) Grandma Albrecht had to do a lot of the outside work. She reportedly had a sore on her leg that wouldn't heal; some think she may have been diabetic. Mother said she thought she had cancer, because she was bleeding before her death. She sometimes came over to the farm and brought toys for the kids.

For some years, the "German Grandma," Wilhelmina (Mina) (actually Mother's aunt) lived with the family. Because her husband was a Civil War veteran, after his death, Mina received a $40 pension check each month. Because she couldn't write, she would sign the check with her "X" and gave it to Mother, who always said that the family wouldn't have made it through the Depression years without that extra income. The older Kehl kids remember Mina as a grumpy old woman who carried a crutch that she used to thump the kids on the head with whenever she got the chance. She reportedly had her favorites—Mel and Carolyn—but Maynard and Mary weren't on that list. Sometimes her sister Mary Haring would come to stay with the family (and she didn't much like Maynard and Mary either, for reasons unknown). My two memories of her were "Granma Soup" (bread and hot water with milk added, which I often requested) and, apparently when I was three, hearing her calling for Annie and running to get Mother, who was out hanging clothes on the line. Mina died in 1939 and was buried in the Massbach Cemetery. I've always regretted that Mary and I, especially, were too young to know and interact with any of our grandparents, thus missing a great deal of generational influence.

Our Parents

Dad attended Sage School to 4th grade. One time at school he had a bad experience: another student got sick, reportedly from eating too much butter, vomited in his hand, and put it in his desk. Dad, not knowing about the vomit, stuck his hand in it (and thereafter he said never liked cooked tomatoes). Grandpa Mike had taught Dad how to fight and defend himself, and he often defended the little kids from bullies. One time he reportedly punched Earl Frederick in the mouth and split his lip open.

Dad courted Mother in his spiffy buggy with a dapper horse, later in his 1912 Model-T, and they were married in November, 1923. (Note that snapshot of him sitting in his buggy, smartly dressed with white shirt, coat, tie, and hat—even the horse seems to be posing!)

Anna Kehl

Mother

Dad with Wolf Pelt

Dad in buggy

Maybe they were encouraged by those other Kehl-Albrecht unions— George and Ella (1914), Chris and Ida (1916), Harry and Lula (1916). (Note that handsome wedding portrait of them.)

Harry & Anna Kehl, Wedding Picture

A year later, they began their family with the birth of Melvin, followed in two years by Maynard, in another two years by John, two years later by Carolyn, three years later by Mary, and three years later by Delmar (where did they get that name—"of the sea" in land-locked Illinois?). (Was I an "accident," as one sibling suggested?) (Mother called me her "little *grutzelei*," roughly translated "scrub.")

Dad with Mel & Maynard

Mother holding Mel & Maynard

*"Granma" (Mother's Aunt, who stayed with us,
holding John, Maynard & Mel standing)*

Carolyn (standing) & Mary (sitting)

Aunt Ella holding Del

Raising six children on a farm through the Depression years was a daunting task, when numerous families lost their farms through foreclosures and others struggled as tenant farmers. (They already had three children before the Crash of '29, the three others born in those formidable thirties.) The older kids remember the story about Dad losing all his money in the bank during the "Crash." He had sold 20 bushels of clover seed for $20 a bushel and had deposited $400 in the bank, a sizeable amount in those days. Two days later the bank closed, and he lost it all. He always thought that the banker knew the doors would close—and thereafter never trusted banks. If he and Mother ordered anything, they always purchased a money order and met the mailman to pay for it. When he traveled to Woodbine to make the payments on the farm at the Federal Land Bank, he always took cash. The "energy and industry" that enabled Anton initially to acquire the farm and Mike to faithfully maintain it enabled Harry and Anna, by grit and the grace of God, to hang onto it during those tough times.

Dad was rather quiet and soft-spoken but an extremely hard worker. He got up early, did the chores, and was out in the field well before most of the neighbors. In the spring, during planting season, and in the fall, during harvest season, he started early and worked late. Though he didn't have much formal education, having dropped out of school to help his father, he was blessed with practical wisdom and good common sense. (For example, he made ice-hooks that could be tied onto overshoes to keep us from slipping after ice-storms.) He ran the steam engine during threshing season as they went the circuit of farms near and far (at one point becoming deathly sick from food poisoning, which, he always maintained, gave him an enlarged heart that he complained of for years). He always took justified pride in his meticulous corn planting, with straight rows so it could be plowed both ways and kept immaculately free of weeds. He was especially conservative, reluctant to change to new ways—from horses to tractors, from threshing-machine to combine, from stacking hay with hay-poles to hay baler, from picking corn by hand to mechanical corn-picker—and reluctant to spend money replenishing the soil with various fertilizers, have a telephone, or hook up to the REA electric line when it finally came through in the late 40's. He was a man of principle and integrity, never working on Sunday, paying his bills on time and in cash, treating other people with deference and himself, all too often, with self-deprecation. He had a reputation for being meticulously honest and a man of his word; if he said he would do something, you could count on it being done.

Dad was skillful at sharpening knives with big whet-stones. After he retired and moved to town, Maynard bought old crosscut saws at auctions, for anywhere from 5 cents to a quarter and gave them to Dad, who loved to make paring knives from the old saw blades. Maynard remembers Dad and the hired man, John Reed, sitting after the chores were done in the evening on the big concrete step on the corn crib, warmed by the afternoon sun, telling stories about threshing, hunting, and other interests until after dark. (One such "snake story" from that oral tradition goes like this: When a man from Pleasant Valley was bitten by a snake, he lived six weeks, but when he'd spit on the ground and the flies would light on that area, they'd drop dead.) After the boys were old enough to work, the hired man was no longer needed.

Mother was loving, patient, and considerate, the "mediator" in the home. She was quiet, especially in a group, but loved visiting one-on-one. To say she was a hard-worker is another understatement. She was very wise, talented, and creative in numerous ways. She (and Rudolph) attended German School for Confirmation. An Award of Honor for perfect attendance at Oakland School, which she received when she was thirteen, attests her scholastic record. Many of the dishes she kept in the glass cupboard she had bought as a girl. She would tell Mary and Carolyn about them as they washed them on various special occasions throughout the year. (The dishes we used growing up were enamel. According to one story Johnny and Carolyn shot at an egg in one of the plates and when Mother found the mark, she hid the B-B gun.)

Mother hated guns because her brother Johnny, when just a boy, accidentally shot and killed a friend when they were shooting birds. Consequently, she was always nervous about our having guns. Uncle Rudy and Louie were given the home farm outside Massbach, but Mother never received anything, even pictures. Only the piano was given to her. Reportedly, some $7,000 given to Chris for a problem he faced was never paid back either.

Mother loved to crochet, tat, and embroider. She made a bedspread, also doilies and other small pieces. Each winter she would make "comforters" for the beds. She would work and card the wool from the sheep they kept for some years (Dad cut his hand shearing them one year), and she made several quilts also. They raised ducks and geese several years, and she would make new pillows from the down. She even made sheets and got bundles of assorted material from Sears to make dresses and also used print feed sacks. There seemed to be nothing Mother could not do—and do it well, everything from cooking to sewing to gardening to painting and wallpapering to being a super-Mother and spiritual influence. She had a good head for business, and many times Dad would call her outside to get her opinion on something he was working on. She usually had a perceptive idea to suggest on how to repair whatever he was working on or building.

All of us kids appreciated her equitable treatment of us; she had no favorites and made every effort to treat us all equally. It was to her that each of us went if we wanted to do something, get something, or go somewhere, and then she presented our case to Dad, who was less accessible and might be expected to deny the request outright ("No, you better not go away tonight; it looks like rain." Or, "You're not going out tonight, are you? It's gonna rain!") If Dad liked someone, he'd do almost anything for him/her, but if he didn't like a person he made no effort to conceal that fact. For some reason, he never cared for Marvin Judas or the Frederick boys and didn't want John and Maynard to associate with them. When John rode away on his motorcycle on Saturday evening, Dad would go up the lane and watch to see if he picked up Marv, so John made sure to go over the crest of the hill before stopping. He also watched to see which direction Maynard went, whether he was driving to the Dinderman place (while dating Bernice, whom Dad especially liked), so Maynard would drive out of his way to thwart the "spying."

It's no judgment to say that Dad tended to be moody and sometimes went for days and sulked without speaking to anyone, so we all had to try to figure out what may have offended him. He often said, "They'll hear you kids over at Judases!" I recall that at one suppertime when we were all talking and laughing, probably at a considerable decibel level, he said, "If you kids don't shut up, I'm gonna go away and never come back." Needless to say, it got very, very quiet—and I, for one, worried about that threat for some time. His naps on the couch were sacrosanct, not to be disturbed. One Sunday afternoon, feeling bored and wanting something to do, I decided to hammer in protruding nailheads on the side of the house. It wasn't long until Dad, awakened from his nap, came out and whupped me with a strip of rubber tube. (I must confess that I pouted for the rest of the day and considered running away from home ....)

Dad loved to listen to the prizefights on the radio on Friday evenings (I recall often falling asleep to Jerry Dunphy describing the blow-by-blow, "brought to you by Gillette Blue Blades, with the sharpest edges ever honed—Look sharp, Feel sharp, Be sharp with the sharpest edges ever honed!"), as well as "Gangbusters," "Mr. District Attorney," "The Great Gildersleeve," "Fibber McGee and Molly," "The Lone Ranger," and others. ("The Lone Ranger," the first episode of which was broadcast in 1933 on station WXYZ in Detroit, was especially popular with Dad and all of us kids; I can recall sitting in front of the radio at 5:30, hearing the rousing strains of Rossini's "William Tell Overture," snacking on a bowl of dry oatmeal.) But Dad didn't like us to have the radio on when he was in the house, especially on Saturday evenings when some of us liked to listen to the WLS National Barn Dance, so we often tried listening softly after he wound the clock and went off to bed—but sometimes that became the source of a mood spell. This is not intended to be an indictment of Dad. He didn't have an easy life, nor did Mother, and they are to be admired and commended for the care they gave us. Dad didn't use profanity, gamble, drink, or carouse. He only occasionally smoked a cigar, and regularly chewed tobacco ('Day's Work," "Beechnut," or "Red Man" in bags or plugs), having begun, he said, as a young man out in the field during long, hot summer days that left his mouth parched. (I recall sneaking some to try once, but the stuff gave me the hiccups for hours, so I settled for chewing prunes or green onions to practice spitting the juice.)

Maynard recalls that Dad would tell the boys how to do something once—and you'd better get it because "You'd get a kick in the butt if you didn't get it right." When he got the Fordson tractors, he said, "They're yours. Take care of them and keep water and oil in them." He had a quick temper and would sometimes stay mad for a week or so, choosing not even to speak to Mother. As kids, the boys learned not to stand around in the house if there was work to be done. Sometimes they'd look out the window to see if Dad were coming. If he came in the front door, the boys would go out the back, maybe into one of the fields or to work on one of the "projects," such as tinkering on a motor or building something.

Neither Dad nor Mother traveled far from the Kehl place. Dad did ride with Dan and Freeman Hanes to Smith Center, Kansas, to visit relatives there. A trip to Chicago was a major travel adventure then, made only a few times in those days—for example, when Mel was in Hines Veteran's Hospital and later, in February, 1957, Mother went to Founder's Week at Moody when Mary was there—and then stayed briefly with Carolyn when Terry was born (accompanied on the train by Cora Rogers). (I still have a postcard she sent me from Chicago: "I enjoyed Founder's week Monday and Tuesday. Now I am here with Carolyn and my new granddaughter. You ought to see her, she sure is a doll. Mrs. Rogers came along out here with me on the Arrow, Monday. Love, Mother") Mother had been repeatedly invited by the Rockford kin to come and stay a few days with them, so after some time, she decided to go—and packed her suitcase with the expectation of visiting with them after one of the reunions—but no one so much as mentioned it, so she came back home, saying nothing to them. (Such disappointments as this may have given rise to her philosophy that "If you don't build up your hopes, you won't be disappointed.")

Without Mother's conservational skills in making do with little, her industriousness in gardening and canning, her creative skills in sewing and mending, her enterprising skills in raising chickens, not to mention her astute advice on the running of the farm, it's doubtful that the farm would have been saved. We always had clean clothes, though often with patches. (At the end of a school day, we always changed clothes, because they had to be worn for a week.) She was a skillful seamstress (I remember going with Mother and Dad to Clinton, Iowa, to get the pedal-pump Singer sewing machine), and she made many of our clothes—for example, the girls' dresses from chicken feed sacks, others from recommissioned hand-me-downs, sheets and towels from flour sacks. (I remember an attractive red shirt she made for me and which I wore one day to high school, but when Darby McGinty said to a group of kids, "Oh, that's pajama material"—though it wasn't true, I never wore it to school again.) She made orders from Sears Roebuck and Montgomery Ward catalogues, and sometimes, after totaling the cost, would erase some of the items. Usually the only income was from the sale of calves and pigs, money which had to last a year until more were ready to sell. Mother also had "egg money" for groceries and other small items, and she sold young roosters and in the fall sold off the old hens when the young pullets started laying. She was always busy from dawn till dark, working in the garden, canning and preparing food, taking care of the chickens, maybe painting or wallpapering (using glue she made from flour and water). She worked long days, staying up late to get all the work done. But she was never too busy to have a talk when one of us came to her for advice or permission to do something or go somewhere. (I recall as a little kid sitting on the floor leafing through her mammoth Martin Luther German Bible, published in Philadelphia in 1856, looking at the pictures and asking her about the stories behind them. She was never too busy to stop what she was doing, come over, read the caption under the picture, translate it, and explain the meaning. Those special instructive moments in the midst of her busy days had a profound influence on me.)

Mother was not only a skillful organizer and manager but also a devout

Christian believer. We can recall her sitting by the battery-powered Philco radio listening to Christian programs from the Moody Station WMBI out of Chicago while she peeled potatoes for supper. She enjoyed the broadcasts of Winona Lake Bible Conference, which she listened to while working around the house, also "The Story" (a daily dramatic enactment of Bible stories) and "Unshackled" (weekly stories about individuals who were converted and their lives miraculously transformed at the Pacific Garden Mission in Chicago. (See more on Christian instruction in Chapter VIII.) Every Sunday afternoon she would read and then write letters to members of the family who were away; then rather than a full meal we often had popcorn (which Dad ground up, added milk, and ate with a spoon) and sometimes popcorn balls.

Ours was a loving family though I don't recall overt expressions or displays of affection between Mother and Dad, except his habit of patting her on the bottom and their going on walks together out in the field to check the growth of corn or oats. Though expressions of love were not voiced, we all knew we were loved. Parental discipline was also firm but reasonable and never excessive. (Mary says she doesn't remember being slapped or spanked by either parent. "I'm sure I deserved it many times, but just a word was enough to make me obey." I recall just one spanking from each parent—the whupping by Dad, mentioned above, and a spanking from Mother when I messed my pants at an age when I should have known better.) They both used verbal rebukes more than physical action. I remember Dad's words, "Oh, you don't want to do that!" And Mother was able to correct undesirable behavior with just a look!

Mother was eleven years younger than Dad, and he lived 21 years after her death. One day in 1942, when I was in first grade, Mother kept Carolyn home because she (Mother) wasn't feeling good (Dad and the boys were doing some work in Loran). Later, apparently, Mother felt even worse, was having a gall bladder attack, thought she was dying, and, not having a telephone, sent Carolyn to school, so the teacher could send someone to call the doctor. Obviously, all of this created quite a stir in the little one-room schoolhouse, and I had no idea what was going on—and no one bothered to tell me or Mary. I just knew that something dreadful must have happened to Mother, Dad, or one of my brothers (those words "something dreadful must have happened" kept going through my mind)—and we didn't learn the truth until after school when we got home.

Mother also had kidney problems and wasn't able to eat salt. Dad insisted that he had an enlarged heart and sometimes complained of being unable to sleep because of a rapid heartbeat. I also remember that he had some back problems (lumbago?) and boils (carbuncles?). Especially scary also was the time when Mother, along with Carolyn, Mary, and I, were hoeing in the garden along the lane when up the road from the south came the Puddle-Jumper with John driving and Maynard holding Dad in the back. It was immediately obvious that he had been hurt. Mother threw down her hoe, cried out "Oh, Harry!" and went running to them. They had been sawing trees, when the trunk of one flew up and hit Dad on the side of his face, shattering the cheek and nose bones, a close call for sure. They put cold cloths on it and called Dr. Petty, who immediately said he should go to the hospital, but, of course, Dad didn't want to, because he had the notion that if you went to the hospital, you likely would never return. He did relent and received good care at St. Francis Hospital in Freeport.

Mother and Dad both lived well and died well. In 1960, what we thought was a fairly routine gall bladder surgery turned out to be extensive cancer. That summer she and Dad had worked together out on the farm, painting the house. Mother remarked that it was one of the best times they had together. Then in the fall she began to feel bad and then worse; visits to the clinic in Freeport and then Monroe, Wisconsin, produced the diagnosis of gall stones. When surgery was performed in January, 1960 (after I had just returned to my teaching job in California), they discovered the cancer and said there was nothing to be done. The last time I saw her alive, I read Psalm 46, which she loved to hear—"God is our refuge and strength, a very present help in trouble ... Be still and know that I am God." The family drove home late that afternoon, each of us quiet, thinking our private thoughts. Maynard stayed and was with her when she passed away. The hymn I remember most vividly from her funeral was that comforting "Rock of Ages, cleft for me; let me hide myself in thee." We knew Mother was with the Lord Jesus in heaven.

It was hard to leave Dad by himself. Mel says Dad was planning to move back to the farm after Mother died, but Mel wisely cautioned him against it, and he changed his mind. He lived in the house on Jackson Street for a number of years and often went over to Aunt Lula's for dinner. Then when he could no longer care for himself, he went to the Good Samaritan Nursing Home, where he passed away in 1981, reportedly having sung "In the Garden" at the top of his voice. Pastor Reser, who visited him just a few days before, assured us that Dad had given evidence of knowing Jesus as his personal Savior.

Centuries ago, Lemuel, in Proverbs 31, wrote the definitive description of and tribute to the worthy woman, so especially well exemplified by Mother:

"She rises while it is still night,
And gives food to her household,
And portions to her maidens ... .
From her earnings she plants a vineyard.
She girds herself with strength,
And makes her arms strong,
She senses that her gain is good;
Her lamp does not go out at night.
She stretches out her hands to the distaff,
And her hands grasp the spindle... .
She is not afraid of the snow for her household,
For all her household are clothed with scarlet.
She makes coverings for herself;
Her clothing is fine linen and purple.
Her husband is known in the gates ... .
Strength and dignity are her clothing,
And she smiles at the future.
She opens her mouth in wisdom,
And the teaching of kindness is on her tongue.
She looks well to the ways of her household,
And does not eat the bread of idleness.
Her children rise up and bless her;
Her husband also ... ,
A woman who fears the Lord, she shall be praised ... .
Let her works praise her in the gates."

We do indeed rise up and call her blessed, as we honor both our mother and our father, as well as our grandfathers and grandmothers, great-grandfathers and great-grandmothers, praising our Heavenly Father for giving us such a Godly heritage.

Extended Family: Aunts, Uncles, Cousins

Uncles, aunts, and cousins make up our "extended family" (or, as someone has waggishly said, the "overextended family"). On Dad's side, of course, we had seven aunts—always a lively group, all relatively short in stature and long on sprightliness!

Ella and George (with the oldest cousin, Frances—they called her "Franny")—and Lula and Harry (with cousins Marjorie, Betty, and Mary) lived in the early years in adjacent houses on the Albrecht homestead before the former moved to a farm in Pleasant Valley and the latter to town in 1944 or 1945. I recall how on one of our rare visits to their house, Uncle George let us play records on a hand-winding Victrola they had and let me look at Bible pictures on a roller viewer.

Chris and Ida (with cousins Lowell and Wilma) lived in Stockton, where Chris had a poultry and egg business. (Ella and Ida were for some time my favorite aunts—I suppose mainly because they paid some attention to me and Ida sometimes brought me candy when they came to visit on the farm.) Cora and Clarence Olds (later Lawrence Knott) lived in Belvedere. (Of all the aunts, I think I knew her least.) Frances and John Baird, Florence and Walter Bailey (with cousins Darlin and Marilyn), Edna and Clyde Shriner (with cousin Donna Jean) all lived in Rockford. (The Rockford kin always seemed to convey, whether consciously or not, that they were somehow superior to the countrified Kehls, with their large family of kids to raise.) I can still hear John Baird's booming, boisterous laugh after he had told one of his jokes or related a detailed account of his latest experiences at the bakery where he worked. I remember riding with him to pick up ice cream at Isenhart's for one of the reunions and another time showing him the steam engine in the machine shed, warning him to be careful not to "cut his foot" on the cow patties. Aunt Florence and "Red" (a house painter) always seemed rather aloof, often just preparing to leave, having gone, or just having returned from Fort Meyers, Florida. Aunt Edna, the youngest, was rather quiet; Uncle Clyde spoke with a slow drawl and flashed a pleasant grin.

On Mother's side we had four uncles—all, at least from a small boy's perspective, rather gruff and taciturn. John and Emma (first wife Lillie) lived on a farm outside Hanover. When Mel left home at eighteen to "work out" (in those days this expression didn't mean "exercising for fitness" but rather "working for wages away from home"), he worked for Uncle Johnny from corn-picking till the first crop of hay, later with Art Beyers Case

Implement and Equipment in Massbach, before he enlisted in the Navy. (I still remember the yummy macaroni salad Aunt Emma made.) Chris and Ida (mentioned above) were both very quiet. Chris loved to fish and seemed to do so at every chance he had. (Mother said Ida had little to say in a group but when it was just the two of them, they had lots to discuss.) Uncle Louie (Ludwig) and Aunt Mary (with cousins Ludwig, Shirley, Kenneth, and Stanley) also lived in Hanover. (I didn't really know them very well either but always felt sorry for Aunt Mary because she was crippled.) Uncle Rudy and Aunt Muriel (with cousins Rudolph, Christiana, Patricia, and John) lived on the Albrecht home place near Massbach. (Rudy was a no-nonsense, rough kind of guy; Muriel—or Merle, as everyone called her—was vivacious and outspoken.)

We seldom got to see aunts, uncles, and cousins, but ordinarily the Kehl kin more than the Albrecht kin. About the only time we saw the Albrechts was at family reunions. We went more often to the Schubert reunion (sometimes held at Krape Park in Freeport or at our house, and once I remember at Charley Schubert's place), later, when it was initiated, to the Kehl reunion, and sometimes to the Albrecht reunion (sometimes held at Old Mill Park in Savanna, at the Albrecht homestead, or at our house). I wasn't especially fond of family reunions, except for the lavish food spread, because, being isolated on the farm and not having much social contact sometimes for weeks at a time in summer, I was painfully shy. And why did aunts and uncles always greet our arrival with, "Oh, is this the baby? Oh, I can't believe this is the baby!" I remember sitting on Dad's lap at Uncle Rudy's, not feeling comfortable going out to play with the cousins. Then, too, I remember a big embarrassment during one Schubert reunion at our house when I was maybe seven or eight: I had my plate filled with all that delicious food—potato salad, macaroni salad, baked beans, dill pickles, sweet pickles, olives, cole slaw, corn, fried chicken, ham, homemade rolls—and was making my way to a seat when I stumbled over one of those %#@^&*#^% croquet hoops in the yard and sent food flying every which way. I think everyone witnessed my fall, and those who tried to be helpful ("Well-l-l-l-l ... We'll getcha some more ..."). On occasions when the reunion was at our house, I guess I was afraid the cousins would break my toys. Selfishly, I didn't realize (or want to realize) how much these rare get-togethers meant to my parents, especially Mother, who seldom got to see her brothers and their families. Sometimes for Albrecht reunions, Dad didn't want to go because he said he was too tired.

For some years the Rockford uncles, aunts, and cousins came to the farm, usually in the fall to get walnuts and hickory nuts and in the spring for strawberries and other fruit. They ordinarily came unannounced and stayed for the weekend. I remember being especially taken with Darlin and Marilyn (who I thought was so pretty) and Donna Jean. At one point we made ice cream and when they saw us taking the ice from the horse tank they said, "Oooh, I'm not gonna eat any of *that*!"—but somehow they later relented. Cousin Lowell, ever the avid sports fan, always tried to get a baseball game going at any gathering.

All seven of the aunts and uncles on Dad's side and all four uncles and aunts on Mother's side have been gone for some years. Of the seventeen cousins on Dad's side, four are gone and of the sixteen cousins on Mother's side, one is gone. I feel I could say to so many of them: "I hardly knew ye!" But which of us could not say with the Psalmist David: "The lines have fallen to me in pleasant places; indeed a goodly inheritance is mine [my heritage is something beautiful]"? Praise the Lord for our wonderful heritage!

III. The Kehl Siblings: We Are Six

"All the brothers were valiant,
And all the sisters were virtuous."
(Inscription in Westminster Abbey)

"How good and how pleasant it is for brothers to dwell together in unity."
(Psalm 133:1)

"Let brotherly love continue." (Hebrews 13:1)

"I am all the daughters of my father's house,
And all the brothers too."
(Shakespeare, *Twelfth Night*)

"Forty thousand brothers
Could not, with all their quantity of love,
Make up my sum."
(Shakespeare, *Othello*)

"Which of us has known his brother? …
Which of us is not forever a stranger and alone?"
(Thomas Wolfe, *Look Homeward, Angel*)

In William Wordsworth's poem "We Are Seven," a little girl is asked how many brothers and sisters she has. She replies, "We are seven," though two are gone away to sea and two lie in the country churchyard: "'How many? Seven in all,' she said." How many Kehl brothers and sisters? We are six. Six in all. God, in His sovereign design, gave each of us five siblings, placed us together in this particular family, each with distinctive DNA, temperament, personality, tendencies, likes and dislikes, abilities, and talents. Three were autumn born (Mel, November 16, 1924; Maynard, September 28, 1926; Del, September 12, 1936), two winter born (John, December 11, 1928; Carolyn, December 5, 1930), one born in spring (Mary, April 9, 1933). Even before He formed us in our mother's womb, He knew us and ordained us (Jeremiah 1:5). We give Him thanks, for we are "fearfully and wonderfully made" (Psalm 139:14).

Sibling Rivalry?

There's been a lot of talk about and books written on sibling rivalry (including Todd Cartmell's *Keep the Siblings, Lose the Rivalry*), but there didn't seem to be much among the six of us. I don't recall any physical fights among us (although I remember that Maynard had a hard, firm fist that could land a real punch on the upper arm). Of course, we had our little tiffs and spats, but nothing major. Maynard tells of John getting angry at something when they were back in the field, as young boys, so Maynard took him down and sat on him, telling him he'd let him up if he could behave himself. From then on they never seemed to have much trouble getting along. They'd sometimes disagree, as we all did at times, but they apparently never fought again.

The three common problems among siblings, according to Cartmell, are name-calling and teasing, using personal possessions without asking, and taking turns with computer video games. Obviously, the third wasn't a problem for us, but name-calling and teasing (or "picking on") were probably the most common. One of the stories often told is about the whine, "Momma, make him leave me alone!" As for name-calling, probably the most unfortunate example was calling Mary "Fatso" or "Fatty." Of course, we all had nicknames for each other, most of them, not surprisingly, originated by first-born Mel. He called Carolyn "Carlager" because when she was in first grade, learning to write in cursive, he said that's what her name looked like. Dad called her "Bape." Maynard's nickname was

"Puss," which, according to Mel, originated from the Tom Mix radio program, which featured a Chinese cook named "Sneezy Snide/Sneezy Puss," so when Maynard would get up in the morning and walk on the cold floor—and sneezed, he got the name "Sneezy Puss," shortened to "Puss." John's nickname was "Runt," apparently because his older brothers thought he was undersized or shorter than they were. For a while, Mel called me "Little Plush" or just "Plush" (maybe reflecting some sibling rivalry?) and also for a while "Dave." Maynard called me "Jake," at least for a while. Mel apparently didn't have a common nickname, although I can remember calling him "Linger," but I have no idea why.

The second most common problem among siblings, according to Cartmell, is using personal possessions without asking permission, but I don't remember this as a real problem among us either. (I recall "borrowing" someone's mittens, getting them all wet in the snow, and being reprimanded. Another time, I wanted to take John's sled to school because I thought it was sturdier and faster than mine.) As noted earlier, the "extra" piece of pie sometimes caused contention among us, but this was well controlled by Mother. I recall that at Christmastime, when Mother made three or four kinds of candy (fudge with walnuts, divinity fudge, taffy, coconut bon-bons), she wisely divided it equally among us. I remember that mine disappeared quite fast, whereas Carolyn stashed hers away (in an old cigar box, as I recall) and kept some for weeks, resulting in covetousness on my part and begging for some of hers.

Probably the relative absence of sibling rivalry among us was due in large part to Mother's equitable treatment of us and the unverbalized ground rules, which, interestingly enough, conform to three suggested by Cartmell: 1) no criticizing, name-calling, or put-downs allowed; 2) respect each other's views; 3) take turns talking. We were taught to respect and value the Kehl family name and each other, because, as Euripides said, "Blood's thicker than water, and when one's in trouble, it's best to seek out a relative's open arms." Or as an old saying puts it, "In time of test, family is best" (well, at least *most* of the time).

Birth Order

Another popular issue concerning siblings is birth order (see, for example, Kevin Leman's *The Birth Order Book: Why You Are the Way You Are*). Leman argues that "in any family, a person's order of birth has a lifelong effect on who and what that person turns out to be." He lists the personal traits, as well as major strengths and weaknesses, of the first-born, middle-born, and last-born. Of course, there are other influential factors, such as the personalities and parenting styles of the parents, the gender of the siblings, the age differences, etc.

First Born

Leman and others who have written on birth order seem to agree that the first-born tends to be a perfectionist, reliable, conscientious, well-organized, hard-driving, a natural leader, critical, highly motivated, goal-oriented, strong-willed, aggressive, precise and even picky, sometimes bossy, wanting to take charge and run the show, a mover and shaker. Many presidents and pastors are first-borns. How many of these traits seem to fit Mel? (You'll have to decide. Wouldn't it be presumptuous of the last-born to attempt an answer to that question?)

Mel tells of how when he was a small boy the hired man Charley Kruse promised him candy if he got the cows, but then put rocks in instead. To get even, he and Maynard put wet corncobs in the exhaust pipe of Charley's car, smiled when he wondered why his engine got hot, then later watched as they came flying out.

When he went to school Mel reportedly spoke as much German as English. The teacher told Mother, "I sure wish I knew what that boy says when he gets angry." Mother said, "It's probably better that you don't."

One time when Mel was mowing with the horses, they began to run away back through the field. The mower ran against a cherry tree and stopped. It ruined the mower (Dad's best), with pieces scattered everywhere, and it tore out the fence. They spent the rest of the day repairing the fence—but Mel was Providentially protected from what could have been a terrible accident!

Mel remembers hunting rabbits and foxes with Dad, Maynard, and John "three hollows west in Nobles." A particular memory was of Dad standing on a brush pile shooting rabbits when they ran out. He also remembers he and Maynard catching fish (carp) by hand in Plum River.

Because of the difference in our ages, Mary and I don't remember very much about Mel. He left home at eighteen to "work out" for Uncle Johnny, then at Beyer's Implements as a mechanic. We remember him bringing the Beyer boys over on their motorcycles—Allen (born the same year and month as Mel), Delbert, and Kelly—and telling stories of their various exploits. (Mrs. Beyer was so friendly; apparently a devout Christian, she always told me she had me on her "prayer list.") (I recall a Saturday evening on the farm, when Mel came by with a carload of girls. What a Casanova or Don Juan he was!) We remember when he came home with the measles, when we were in grade school. We were all quarantined and had to miss quite a bit of school that year. (I recall sitting in the room upstairs, when he was in bed, and "entertaining" him, crawling up in the attic, etc.) I recall Mother and Dad's surprise and concern when Mel told them he had enlisted in the Navy (the same time as Delbert Beyer, but they stayed until haymaking was done). When he went to Chicago for his physical, he learned that he is color-blind. (He was told, "If you get two more guys, we'll send you to the Marines.) When he went off for basic training at Great Lakes and then to the U. S. Naval Dry Dock at Hunter's Point, near San Francisco, he was the hero of us all. We wrote to him, and I still have several postcards I received from him. (One postmarked July, 1944, reads: "Hi Dave: Here is a card for you. I am o.k. Nice place out here. Don't get cold in the winter. Write me a letter." Another card had a cartoon showing a busty gal with sailors' names tattooed on both arms, the caption reading, "She was true—but didn't say who!"). Mother got a banner with a star ("Serving Our Country") to hang in the north room window. When Mel came home on furlough, Mother invited all the aunts, uncles, and cousins to come for a big dinner celebration.

In February, 1947, Mel announced his marriage to Dorothy Foley, who seemed to be a gracious person (she sent me boxes of comic books, which I read and kept for a long time—and gave me my first Kodak Brownie camera for Christmas). After his discharge, he and Dorothy drove back, along with Butch, their little dog (in time for Maynard and Bernice's Ice Cream Supper, 1948). Initially, they lived in the downstairs bedroom of the farmhouse, and Mel worked for Moltmann and Smith Ford, then at the "Proving Ground" (Savanna Ordnance Depot), later buying the house on Galena Street, and later still running his own auto repair shop on the south edge of town. Dorothy introduced us kids to Monopoly, which we loved to play for hours (she often seemed to gloat over her accumulation of houses and hotels). She demonstrated "how a match burns twice"—at Mary's expense. (The girls sought revenge by wrapping up a box of walnuts for the pet squirrel, with a sign reading "Nuts to you," initially mistaken for a box of candy.) She also drove the tractor (Allis-Chalmers) when we were baling hay (sometimes, reportedly, intentionally driving close to the bushes at the edge of the field so they would brush John or Maynard on the baler (when it was still necessary for two men to ride on the baler, one to push the wires through so the other one could tie them). In June, 1951, we welcomed Jackie (Gladys) Ewing into the family—and subsequently their children, Judy, Karl, and Dawn (and were saddened by Karl's tragic death at 25).

Mel has been a fine older brother, as first-born demonstrating influential strengths of leadership, commanding respect, being goal-oriented, hard-driving, and enterprising. We connected on several different levels, from our mutual admiration for the music of Eddy Arnold (the "Tennessee Plowboy," who passed away in May of 2008) to our appreciation of books about sea adventures, such as *Mister Roberts*.

Mel & Wife Jackie.

Mel & Jackie with Karl, Judy, Dawn

Middle-Borns

Perhaps one of the weaknesses of the birth order studies is that they seem to make few distinctions between or among the middle-borns. In our case, there are four middle-borns, two males and two females, with seven years separating the oldest and youngest. Leman says, "When you say 'middle child,' think contradictions … . Middle borns are a bit mysterious … Any time a second-born child enters the family, his life-style is determined by his perception of his older sibling." According to the research, the middle-born is a mediator, compromising, diplomatic, independent, avoids conflict, has many friends, is loyal to peers, is secretive, a maverick, unspoiled, has fewer hang-ups or problems than the first-born or only child. How many of these characteristics seem to fit Maynard, John, Carolyn, and Mary? To what extent did they "grow up feeling squeezed and rootless"? Did they learn to be "realistic, unspoiled, maybe rebellious because they felt they didn't fit in"? (Of course, Mel, like most first-borns, always said that Maynard and John got away with a lot more than he did.) Did "being treated unfairly make them suspicious, cynical, even bitter"? Do they at times "appear to be bullheaded, stubborn, unwilling to cooperate"? (Again, I'll pass on answering those questions posed by the researchers.)

Second Born

As the story goes, it was a dark, cold, rainy night in late September when Maynard came into the world. The dirt roads had turned to mud. Dr. Ray Petty, who was called for the delivery came with his driver, Raymond Dietricht, as far as Plum River. While the doctor was at the house all night, his driver, waiting in the car during that cold night, thought he'd freeze.

Maynard was the self-admitted passive brother. Of course, as children growing up on the farm, all of us were very bashful. When someone stopped by the farm, we often ran and hid, then peeked out through the curtains. As noted above, Maynard and Mel spoke as much German as English when they started school, and perhaps the teachers were hard on them because of it.

The story is told about one time the family went to visit Grandpa Mike and Grandma Caroline in town. Mel and Maynard went outside to play. Mel, age 4, was to keep an eye on his brother. Maynard wandered down to the bottom of the hill, where a man found him. When Dad and Mom asked where Maynard was, Mel didn't know. When Maynard was safely returned to his parents, they learned that a stranger had picked him up and took him down to the sheriff's office, not knowing whose child he was. He told the family that the boy was "like a wildcat," kicking and scratching, screaming and hitting, trying to get away.

Another time, when Dad, Mom, and Maynard (only a year old) were riding in the old Model-T truck to deliver some oats that Dad owed Uncle Rudy, something broke on the magneto (which was on the outside) and it stalled. Mother and Maynard had to sit in the car all day, waiting for Dad to get it going. Still another time, when Maynard was 2 or 3, he was riding in the Model-T truck with Dad and Grandpa Mike back in the field. When Dad got out to open the gate, leaving the truck running, the emergency brake didn't hold, and the truck ran down over the hill. Grandpa Mike bailed out and Maynard was thrown through the windshield, receiving cuts on his chin and by his eye. (The cab was a homemade one, with window glass for the windshield.) Mother had to come back and help Dad get the truck out of the ditch. (Grandpa Mike didn't know how to drive.)

From about the age of six, the boys had chores to do and they worked in the field, first with horses and later driving the Fordson tractor. When they came home from school they would have to go to the woods to cut up, with a crosscut saw, the trees that Dad had cut down during the day. In four or five days, they'd have enough wood cut to last the winter and into the summer for cooking. Later Dad would have three or four men come to help cut the wood into chunks with a buzz saw. Still later the chunks would be split and thrown onto a huge pile, ready to be carried into the house for firewood. During harvest time, the boys had to help pick corn by hand. As it was picked, it was thrown on piles down the row; then someone would drive the tractor and wagon along while the others picked up the piles of corn and threw it on the wagon. Sometimes they didn't get all the piles picked up before the snow came, and they would have to dig it out of the snow, a cold, wet job.

None of the kids had many toys to play with. Maynard and Mel each had a big truck that Grandma Albrecht had given them. Later Dad and Mother gave Mel a tricycle; the next year they gave the trike to Maynard, and Dad gave Mel a new wagon. Maynard and John had a pair of boxing gloves to play with. The boys made much of their own fun. For example, they had a pet rooster. Once they tied a string on a mouse and fed it to the rooster; when the rooster swallowed it, they'd pull it back out. They continued to feed the mouse to the rooster until it wouldn't eat it anymore. (Uncle Clyde Shriner, who was visiting at the time, was really entertained by all of that.) At age 14 Maynard sent away to Hills Brothers Outfit for a knife (which he kept all his life). He paid $5 or $6 for it. (He could buy knives with a single blade at the dime store for 10 cents, but he'd lose them as fast as he could buy them.) Maynard and John had a pigeon pen (in the area where Mike's trailer is) and had one pigeon almost totally white. Crows made much better pets than pigeons, however, and Elmer the crow was distinctive. Elmer loved to snitch and hide screws and other small items, to sneak up on the tomcat and peck his tail, to imitate chickens and take a bath in the chickens' water (until a cranky setting hen came along). He reportedly predicted changes in the weather, sitting on the windmill making all kinds of noises. Someone said that if you split the tongue, a crow could learn to talk like a parrot, but that never came about. Maynard did teach Elmer to sit on his head. Once when John drove the Model-A truck to a neighbor's house, Elmer hopped out from underneath and strutted around, pretty as you please.

Mel, Maynard, and John improvised with an old buggy, steering it down the hill toward the mailbox and up the next hill past Judases to school. One time they were taking pumpkins to school to make jack-o-lanterns, when the steering chain broke, they ran off the road, and turned over, scattering pumpkins all over.

At an early age, Maynard would crawl through the window of the shop to get old nails or whatever he could find to use to make something. Once he took an old phonograph up in the weeds behind the shop to fix it. The spring was broken, so he fixed that. He figured that since broken things were of no use anyway, it wouldn't hurt to take them apart and see if they could be fixed. (Bernice always said he was born with a monkey wrench in his hand.) Maynard made a power lawn mower, using a Maytag washing machine motor advertised in *The Mirror Democrat*. He was also good at baking cookies and cakes, and loved making taffy (until the war, when sugar was scarce).

Maynard, oldest of the middle-borns, has distinguished himself especially for his independent thinking, being "willing to do things differently, take a risk, strike out on his own" (Leman). He and John were especially close, doing many things together. (The story of how John reported that Maynard "has sand on his feet" is recounted in "Remembrance of Things Past: Sibling Dialogue," Chapter IV.) For example, they tried growing peanuts (down where Mike's trailer now sits), and Maynard made a bean and peanut huller. They also raised potatoes and made root beer. Maynard made a water wheel in the ditch below the house and enjoyed watching it spin when it rained and water ran in the ditch. He also constructed a dam below that.

Maynard seemed to have a natural mechanical ability and electronic genius, constructing a wind-charger, installing the light plant, wiring the house (I recall being recruited to crawl under the floor to help him get a wire through, having to grit my teeth on my claustrophobic feelings).

Maynard and Mel learned to ride bicycle on Route 78. The bike belonged to the Frederick boys. They'd take turns riding, and the rest would run along behind, riding all the way to Pleasant Valley. For some reason, John never learned to ride, maybe because he never got a turn? Mother was reportedly very upset with them when she found out they were riding on the road and said they could have been killed.

We remember the stories about the ear surgery Maynard had as a child. While growing up, he was also prone to pneumonia (having it once as a young child and later when he was around eighteen or nineteen), and we remember the smell of the onion poultice that Mother made to put on his chest. (Maynard says it felt like a 200-pound man on his chest, and he couldn't wait for Mother to get back after warming the poultice.) It may sound like an "old wives' tale" panacea, but apparently it worked (also for grandchildren Barb, Kathy, and Linda when they were sick). (Also maybe the Sloans liniment, Carter's Little Liver Pills, castor oil [ugh] and cod liver oil, Vicks VapoRub, Smith Bros. Coughdrops, and McNess Elixir used while we were growing up were also effective.) Maynard was also susceptible to poison ivy and poison oak (as John was allergic to bee stings); he only had to get in its vicinity and he would break out. (I also recall when he broke his arm trying to crank the Model-T.) We enjoyed riding in the rumble-seat of his Model-A.

Stories have been told of how Maynard used to climb in the clothes room window when doors were locked and he got home late (or early in the morning—sometimes when Dad was getting up). Mel and John have told how Maynard would delay doing his chores (milking a cow) because he would be listening to "The Lone Ranger" or "Jack Armstrong." He would get his coat, cap, and overshoes on, have his milk bucket in hand, then sit and listen. Mother would say, "Go milk the cow," and he would say, "As soon as the story's over," but then would stay for the next and the next until it was pitch-dark.

Maynard's first job was working for Ralph Frederick, repairing cars, tractors, engines. He went to wherever people had machines to work on, carrying his tools along. Many times he worked all day without lunch. Sometimes he and his brothers were paid for their work, but sometimes they never received any remuneration at all.

We welcomed Bernice Dinderman into the family in April, 1948 (with a notable shivaree, or charivari, if you prefer, and well-attended ice cream supper that followed) and subsequently their children Barbara (the first grandchild/niece—how exciting it was to see her take her first steps), Jean, and Linda. Maynard and Bernice lived six months "on the hill." Bernice's father died suddenly in 1948, and they moved in with her mother to help her prepare the farm for sale. Maynard then worked for Jim Keckler, farming, for a "salary" of $100 a month—and lunch. In 1948, they moved to the Ray Bashaw farm, working for half-shares of the grain and animals and were furnished the house. After purchasing the farm in 1959, they completely remodeled the house, room by room, including plumbing for running water (1963), installation of bathroom (1973), rewiring, and heating system. The house was in deplorable condition when they decided to move there, and Bernice initially thought it was impossible to repair, but she said, "Never tell him he can't fix anything—because he always can and did." His motto was: "You can do anything you put your mind to." Pretty much a self-taught man, once he saw something he could picture it in his mind—a photographic memory. He attended R.E.T.S. (Radio, Electronic, Television School) in Rock Island, graduating in 1966.

Maynard supplemented his income by repairing machinery for the Green Giant Canning Factory in Lanark, worked shortly at Burgess Battery in Freeport, at the Herman Nelson/American Air Plant in Morrison, at Atwoods in Stockton, then for twenty-four years as maintenance electrician at Kelly-Springfield Tire Company in Freeport. During all those years working away from home, he continued to farm full-time, raising beef cattle and corn, oats, and hay. Maynard has also been a fine older brother, one who could repair or fix just about anything, one who has been reliable, trustworthy, true-blue loyal.

Maynard & Wife Bernice

Maynard & Bernice with Barbara, Jean, Linda

Third Born

The second middle-born sibling was John, to whom we three younger siblings felt closer because we were closer in age. Leman's designations of being "unspoiled, realistic, a peacemaker, willing to work things out, great at seeing issues from both sides, diplomatic" seem to fit John well. He was not only a fine brother but also a great friend. Note the snapshot taken at Aunt Ella's with Mother on the left holding me as a baby, Mary seated on a chair, Carolyn to her left, Maynard sitting on the ground (making one of his common "snoot" faces, John standing behind him looking back over his shoulder at Mother and me. Or note the one of the six of us, with John holding baby-me, everyone looking fairly pleasant.

Mother holding Del, with Aunt Edna and Florence, Mary seated, Carolyn, John looking back at Del, Maynard making his typical picture face

The six Kehl siblings

Mother said John requested to share a room with me, and through the years he proved very sensitive, understanding, and patient with all my foibles (bedwetting, waking up at night thinking wrinkles in the sheets were snakes, my strange dreams, fears about someone breaking in to kill us all, etc.). John was also my protector or defender—at least on one occasion when, as a first grader, I was walking home from school and Willard (Billy) Nowak, who had been picking on me, started shoving and punching me as we approached our drive—and John came running out, beat him up, and sent him home with a bloody nose and black eye. (After that, Billy was quite friendly, often asking me to identify words at school and help him with his reading.) (When I asked John in 2004 about this incident, he said he didn't remember it.) Maynard and John were considerate of their younger siblings. On one occasion, after poking around in a junk-ditch, they brought home for me a little tricycle, which I valued and spent many hours playing on.

John and Maynard trapped together for muskrats, minks, foxes, and coons to earn some money of their own. During the war years the ceiling price for muskrat was $3 to $4, $15-16 for fox pelts, and mink up to $40. Sometimes the boys would get up to 16 a winter. Crow heads were worth 10 cents each, the bounty paid by the county. The boys trapped along Plum River from the Loran Road to State Highway 78, plus the little creeks that branched off. It was difficult and very cold walking along the river bank in the deep snow—before school. They marked their traps with sticks and had to wade out to check them. They boiled their traps in walnut hulls (after the walnuts were placed on the calf stable roof to dry and then run through the corn sheller to get the hulls off) to remove the human smell and better disguise them. The Frederick boys wanted to trap the same area, so Dad suggested that the Kehls trap one side of the river and the Fredericks the other side, a solution that seemed to work well. According to one story, Floyd Frederick had tried to catch a mink for some months; Maynard and John set their traps—and the next day had the mink Floyd had been trying to catch. They kept their skinned and stretched pelts in the downstairs north bedroom, which stayed quite cool in winter. They sold their furs to Sears or to a buyer who came in to Woody Johnson's feed store. They also hunted, shooting foxes and crows and rabbits, squirrels, and pheasants to eat (deer were rare in the area at that time.)

Dad, with Mel, Maynard, & John, & wolf pelts

Besides trapping and hunting, they also tried spelunking, exploring a cave they found back in Cooney's timber, apparently rappelling down part of the way on a rope—which Mother and the rest of us heard about *after* the fact. Another hobby was making homemade firecrackers, using a Model-T sediment bowl with blasting powder and fuse. How could anyone say the Lord was not watching over this family?

And, of course, there were the motorcycles. All three of the older boys had motorcycles. Dad gave Mel $45 to buy an old red Harley 28 he saw in a parking lot in town, but it was nothing but trouble. They would tinker on it all week and then be able to ride it only a couple of hours on Sunday before it broke down again. John's favorite expression was: "It never was any good!" Maynard bought an Indian 25 a few years later, for $15. It was all torn apart and he brought it home in a peach basket in the back of his Model A coupe, put it back together, and rode it a lot. Maynard planted corn on a 12-acre field at Tiptons one year and after harvesting and selling it was able to buy a new 1947 Harley for $850. He and John ordered cycles from a dealership in Clinton, Iowa, paying $25 down for each. When the first one came in, Maynard let John have it. Maynard's arrived several months later. John's was black, Maynard's red: they didn't choose a color when they ordered, just took what came in. Maynard's cost more because it had a windshield, saddlebags, spot light, and luggage carrier—plus chrome wheels (nowadays it would be called "a full dresser"). Maynard shared, letting John have one chrome wheel (probably receiving a candy bar for it, chocolate being Maynard's pay for things). John drove Maynard down to pick his up, accompanied by Bernice. While Maynard was inside paying for the cycle, John and Bernice took a ride around Clinton, and then she rode back to Mt. Carroll in the car with John instead of on the cycle with Maynard.

Maynard and John each had a leather motorcycle jacket (a gift from Mother and Dad, probably for Christmas) and wide leather belts with zip pockets. (Maynard had his jacket all his life, but his leather hat, which he wore for years, was stolen.) When Maynard and John were "running around" during their teen years, they'd ride their Harleys to town. When it was time to go home, they'd ride up Cemetery Hill and head out of town on Route 78. There was a cranky old woman who lived on Cemetery Hill who was irritated by the noisy motorcycles going through her neighborhood, so she called the city policeman (Charles "Coxie" Petty). The boys were not malicious and wouldn't have intentionally agitated her, but when she called the police, they were irritated, so every time they left town, they rode up Cemetery Hill and through the lady's neighborhood. According to Maynard, "We'd light it at half-throttle a ways and then open those cycles up and head out of town!" (taking the street past Good Samaritan Center on the north edge of town and hit Route 78). By the time she called the police and he got over to that part of town, they'd be nearly home.

In the summer of 1950, it was a baby instead of a cycle. Mother expressed her concern about the danger of the three—Maynard, Bernice, and Barb—riding on the motorcycle (he even got a side car but it was hard to balance), so he sold the cycle in 1954. John kept his for some years after that, and Mother was concerned about Dad riding on the back, especially after they hit a dog coming north on Highway 78 but escaped injury, another evidence of God's protective grace.

John drove Mary and me to high school our first year before the bus came out our way and before I was old enough to drive. Though he had to interrupt what he was doing in the field, I never once heard him complain. We also rode with him to church at times. We were pleased when he dated Agnes Rogers, who had been Mary's friend from the church even before they dated, and we welcomed Agnes into the Kehl family in March of 1951, and later Edna Wilson in April of 2002, a special friend. John and Agnes lived briefly in two of the bottom rooms of the farmhouse after they were married, then in town while John worked for Law's Turkey Farm. We were especially close to their children—Mike, Debbie, and Kathy, whom we sometimes kept and enjoyed playing with.

John was a fine older brother whom I have long appreciated. I enjoyed riding with him on his '47 Harley-Davidson motorcycle. He was always a big tease, with a great sense of humor. I've always admired his ability to fix just about anything but even more his strong Christian faith and commitment to serving the Lord as elder, deacon, trustee and Sunday School teacher. In November, 2004, as I was driving from O'Hare to Mt. Carroll for John's funeral, I was meditating on the life John and I had shared, when suddenly it stopped snowing and a spectacularly beautiful sunset lit up the western sky. I had been thinking of how as a little kid I could never fall asleep on Saturday nights until John got back home from his outings and came riding (or coasting with the engine off) down the lane on his Harley or his '49 Ford. As I admired the sunset, it was as if our Heavenly Father was communicating to me, "John is home. You can rest assured. Carry on the work he cared about so much."

John & Wife Agnes

John with family

John & Edna

Fourth Born

As I think about sibling influence, I realize that each one influenced me in certain respects, but Carolyn had a particular, significant influence. Before I started to school, I asked her to bring books home for me, which she did faithfully, and when she started to high school and had access to the public library, again she brought books home for me. (I remember in particular *Smokey* by Will James, *Hans Brinker and the Silver Skates*, *The Little Shepherd of Kingdom Come*, and others.) And she read stories to me. I remember my favorite, which I requested over and over again ad nauseam—"Billy Bantam" (about a "cocky" bantam rooster who taunted a predatory fox by letting the fox get close, then flying out of reach on the roof of the chicken house. The wily fox determined to "pile rock upon rock, stone upon stone" until he could climb up and grab the rooster—but after toiling for hours and when he was almost to the top, the rooster pushed the pile over and the fox went tumbling down, vowing to try again another day). (Another favorite was one about an elderly couple who bake a gingerbread boy, who decides to run away, is chased by the couple and, in turn, by a dog, cow, and horse—each time he says, "I've run away from a couple, a dog, a cow, and I can run away from you too!" Finally, when he gets to a river with no bridge, he makes a deal to get a ride across on the back of an alligator, who gobbles him up in midstream.)

Here, in her own words, are two special events she recalls.

"Mail Service to the Farm"

We lived on R.R. #4, also known as RFD #4. (R.R. stands for Rural Route and RFD is Rural Free Delivery.) Our mailman was Winsel McGrath. Our mailbox was at the bottom of the hill toward the school because the route did not go past the farm. On school days, we took the mail home after school. Saturdays and during the summer, I usually went for the mail. In the winter after a snowstorm and the milk truck came through, the tracks were wide enough for the sled. It was a great ride down, but going home meant pulling the sled up the hill.

A first-class letter cost 3 cents, and postcards were 1 cent. To mail a letter, we put three pennies in a strip of cloth and tied it around the letter. The mailman bought the stamps at the post office in town and mailed the letters. In the spring and during the winter months when the roads were impassable, the mailman did not attempt to deposit mail in our mailbox. Our mail was delivered at the property line between our farm and Schmidts'.

In the fall after Mother sold the roosters to Johnston Feed in town, she ordered our winter clothes from Montgomery Ward and Sears, Roebuck catalogs. A credit card was unheard of in those days. The merchandise was paid with a postal money order. The mailman purchased the money order and mailed the order, which was shipped from Chicago. It was my duty to meet the mailman when we sent an order with cash. One fall I had over $100 in cash, a lot of money in those days, for the order to Montgomery Ward (or maybe Sears, Roebuck). I walked across the fields beyond the "ole house holler" to meet the mailman. When I arrived at the property line, I realized I had lost the order *and* the cash. I retraced what I thought was my path through the harvested oats field. It was a challenging task, as the stubbles were the same color as the envelope containing the order and cash. I *had* to find that envelope! I searched for the lost envelope, praying and crying all the way. It was a miracle that I found the envelope, but I missed the mailman. I didn't tell Mother that I had lost the money, only that I had missed the mailman, which was the truth. The next day I met the mailman and the order was on its way. I was so thankful that I had found the money. I believe it was an answer to prayer.

We trusted a dedicated mailman with the cash, but those days are gone; it's a different world we live in today. It's risky to mail money in any form in the neighborhood mailbox or the box attached to the residence. Identify theft is a common occurrence. I take my mail to the post office and hope no one goes "postal" before my mail reaches its destination. In my opinion, those were "the good ole days" when life was much less complicated. People were more trusting and neighborly. Could it be that is just the way it was in rural areas, or because I was a kid and now I see things as an adult? Maybe.

"High School"

As long as I can remember I wanted to be a nurse, which meant having a high school education. The summer after graduating from eighth grade, we painted the house. The storm shutters were to be painted a dark green. I'm not sure how that job fell to me. It was a tedious job, but as I worked I tried to figure out how I could get to town to attend high school. Dad was adamant about not allowing me to board in town, even though I could probably have stayed at Aunt Lula's. He seemed to think that any young girl who stayed away from home got pregnant.

The new teacher for the coming school year at Sage School was Mrs. Florence Elliott. She did not drive, so her husband, who worked at the Mt. Carroll hardware store, was going to drive her out and pick her up at night. Bingo! Maybe I could ride in with him in the morning and ride out at night. Mother, Dad, and I went to see the Elliotts in Mt. Carroll. I don't know what the agreement was, but I'm certain there was some compensation. Mr. Elliott never went one inch out of his way for me. He never dropped me off at school. I walked from the downtown hardware store to school and to and from Sage School when the weather was nice. When it rained or was snowy, I walked a mile to the top of the hill just off the cement road, Highway 78.

After the first year, Dad, Maynard, or John did the driving. After school I stayed in the library until closing. Sometimes I went to the Court House to go to the bathroom. Many nights I sat outside on the steps waiting for my ride home. When Maynard drove in the morning, I was *always* late for school. He would stop at Gambles or Western Auto before taking me to school. I wondered many times if I would get to school faster if I just walked from downtown. Many evenings, John played pool with Ray Moshure (I had a crush on him). Females were not allowed in the pool hall, so I had to sit in the car and wait and wait!

I'm very thankful for the opportunity to get an education, although I didn't become a professional nurse. The hospital refused my admission application due to a physical condition. Becoming the mother of four children gave me practical experience in dealing with broken bones, broken teeth, ear infections, bronchitis, impetigo, scrapes, cuts and bruise. I've made many mistakes during my lifetime, because I'm imperfect. When I was young I didn't know the future, and I don't know it now. I do, however, know who holds my future—Almighty God! [End of Carolyn's account].

Mary says she and Carolyn were quite close when young, and often played house together. Mother would "stamp" pillowcases for them to embroider. Carolyn liked to be outside, and Mary stayed close to the house, learning to bake and sew. The story is told of how the two of them, neither one very old at the time, went in the hen house, gathered the eggs, and threw them out against the hog house to see them break and run down the wall. Later, when Mother went to gather the eggs, she couldn't believe she wasn't finding many, but when she got to the back door, she saw where the eggs had gone! Another story deals with how Carolyn was supposed to help Mary bake a cake. Mary knew the "one egg" recipe by heart, but this day they were making a different one. The eggs were to be separated, the whites to be beaten and added last, but apparently Carolyn didn't read the recipe to Mary, who was too small to read, so they forgot to add the egg whites. The cake rose and then fell flat like a pancake. When they took the "cake" out of the oven, Mother, Dad, and the brothers, who had been digging potatoes, laughed but ate it nevertheless.

There's also the story about Carolyn and her pet chick. It was one of the little chicks from a large brood and it couldn't find the right hen, so Carolyn adopted it and played with it, then put it in one of the planter boxes of the corn planter in the shed—and forgot all about it. Finally, the next day she remembered where she had put it—and recovered it just in time.

In addition to the influence of books and the love of reading, Carolyn and I shared our dreams for the future. I recall our being out in the blackberry patch behind the granary picking berries but at the same time sharing what we wanted to do with our lives. We both knew we wanted to go on to high school and then to college, even then realizing that education provided a way to get beyond the provincialism of country and small-town life, the so-called "village virus." Carolyn wanted to be a nurse—and she would have made a good one. I recall Mother and Dad, Carolyn, Mary, and I going to Freeport to check on her nurses training. We were all disappointed when she was told that because of her heart murmur, she wouldn't be accepted in the nursing program. (I wish they had checked other programs.) She went to work at McKinley and Hummelgards in Clinton until she had enough money saved to enroll at Moody Bible Institute in Chicago, then to Bob Jones University for a year and a half to work on a teaching certificate. We welcomed Gerald Anderson (subsequently Herman Ameen and Cliff Moses) into the family, and their four children: Terry, Robert, James and Lonnie. Carolyn has been a fine big sister, manifesting some of the traits of first-borns, such as being goal-oriented, hard-driving, conscientious, and strong-willed.

Loni Anderson and son, Alexander

Terry and Brianna Felix

James and Linda Anderson, Abigail,
John and Sabrina

Robert and Thaworn Anderson

Carolyn Kehl (Mother)

Carolyn & Family

Fifth Born

The youngest of the middle-born siblings is Mary, certainly manifesting Leman's traits of being "unspoiled and realistic, having reasonable expectations," maybe "growing up feeling squeezed and rootless," maybe "being a bit suspicious, cynical, even bitter" as a result of feeling she was treated unfairly at times.

A story involves the flowerbed Maynard and John had behind the granary. Mary, who wasn't very old, used to go in and pick the flowers, so the boys, including Mel, decided to play a trick on her: they put a pail of water above the gate and fixed it so that when the gate opened, the water spilled. Then they had Carolyn get Mary to go in and pick the flowers, while they hid to watch. Apparently, the trick worked to perfection, but Mary didn't share the mirth.

It was Carolyn and Mary's job to wash and dry the dishes. One time Mary dropped a bowl and a piece hit her foot, causing extensive bleeding—and great concern in the family. As I recall they wrapped it in dish cloths until it finally stopped. Mary recalls not being able to go with the family to a funeral because she didn't have boots, but generally we didn't suffer want, though we may not have liked the "hand-me-down" system.

Another story is about how Mary, Carolyn, and Bernice (then around 11) took some leftovers down to the arch-cellar. There they saw John and Marv's root beer and drank two bottles, an infraction for which Maynard and Ralph (Frederick) were blamed.

Because we were closer in age, Mary, Carolyn, and I spent more time together, and by the time I was born, the older boys were out in the field and didn't have time to play with younger siblings. The three of us sometimes took the little coaster wagon on "picnics" down to "the old house hollow" or down to "the branch." I remember playing store, making mud pies and mud shakes, or delivering "the mail" in the wagon. One of our fond memories was looking for morel mushrooms in spring back in "the timber" by the sandbank or going flower-picking for Mother's Day (violets, buttercups, blue bells, Johnny-jump-ups), sometimes over to Tiptons. Mary and I were especially close when we were in high school and studied together (see Chapter VI, "Telling Tales Out of School"). Because no buses ran to our place, the plan was for Mary to learn to drive and get her license, so I could get a permit and drive us to school. I attempted for some time to teach Mary to drive the Model-A, but each time she let out the clutch, she'd kill the engine, so finally, fearing that the clutch was in jeopardy, it was decided that John would drive us to school and pick us up in the afternoon (ordinarily we waited in the library until he arrived). Later we rode the bus (first to be picked up, last to be dropped off) and the following year I drove the Model-A (with Marian Judas as another passenger).

John in Model A Ford

Mary and I connected on a number of interests—for example, our appreciation of country/western music, particularly the WLS National Barn Dance, which came on for three hours every Saturday night, featuring such performers as Lulu Belle and Scotty ("Have I Told You Lately That I Love You?"), Rex Allen, Captain Stubby and the Buccaneers, Granpa Jones, Little Jimmy Dickens ("Take an Ole Cold Tater and Wait"), and others. Sometimes, as noted above, we had to turn the radio way down low and strain to listen because Dad didn't approve. In addition, for a while, we listened to a cowboy singer (Gene Evans) in Clinton and went to meet him and got his autograph. With money I had saved up, mainly from collecting copper and brass, I bought records by Eddy Arnold ("Make the World Go Away"), Roy Acuff, Roy Rogers, Gene Autry, Sons of the Pioneers, etc.

When Mary graduated from 8th grade, Mother was not well, so Mary was kept home to care for her and do the household duties. (Dad had to get papers signed, because it was stipulated that kids had to attend school until age 16.) When I entered high school, Mary was able to enroll also. She also had experience working one summer for Herb and Mary Kessler as cook and housekeeper, later at the Trickle Inn Drive-In and still later at the Swiss Cheese Factory in Milledgeville, before attending Moody Bible Institute for three years. When she graduated she moved to Ohio, where she worked with the Binkleys, helping in the Church of God at Tabor. She met Ken Clouser, who was pastor of the church in Neptune, and in June, 1960, we welcomed Ken Clouser into the family and subsequently their two children, Roger and Natalie. They moved to Harrisburg, Pa. in 1962 and have lived in Middletown, Pennsylvania ever since.

Mary & Family (Ken, Chris, Natalie)

Joe, Natalie, Noelle, Chris

Mary has been a fine older sister—trustworthy, unspoiled, diplomatic, hard-working, conscientious. She's a talented cook and baker, an artist who works with food rather than with words or paint, reminding me of a character in Anne Tyler's *Dinner at the Homesick Restaurant*, who creates "masterpieces" of food—"It's *not only* pot roast ... This is something more. I mean, pot roast is really not the right name; it's more like ... what you long for when you're sad and everyone's been wearing you down ... It's a consoling pot roast ... There was something tender, almost loving, about [her] attitude toward people who were eating what [she'd] cooked them ... He asked her for another slice of pie." Ah, yes, wouldn't a big slice of Mary's peach, berry, apple, or cherry pie hit the spot right now? Or maybe some cobbler or cookies (snickerdoodles, chocolate chip, or raisin-filled)? Mary, like Mother in this respect, has been a "feeder," a nurturer.

Last Born

As for the last-born child, the research has shown that "the baby" tends to be charming, manipulative, blaming others, an attention seeker, often loves the limelight, tenacious, a people person, precocious, engaging, affectionate, a natural salesperson. (I'm not sure how many of those fit. Go ahead, decide on your own; have a field day!) Leman does make several statements that seem to apply remarkably well. For example, he says, "Last borns are on a seesaw of emotions and experiences they find hard to explain or understand." Again he writes, "Last borns are used to being put down or written off…. It's no wonder that the last born grows up with an 'I'll show them' attitude … " (I remember wanting to go with Maynard and John and one of their friends on a motorcycle ride, but was told, "You'd better stay here; you're too little." Another time, at one of the county fairs, I wasn't permitted to go into a particular tent with the others because the exhibit was only for "mature adults," so I had to wait outside.) Leman says further, "The older kids always laugh at the babies, who still grope blindly with fantasies like Santa Claus and the Tooth Fairy." These fantasies were never emphasized at our house, certainly not the Tooth Fairy, but one Easter an older sibling, John, I think, enticed me into running to the window in an attempt to see the Easter Bunny ("Oh look, there goes the Easter Bunny!")

Leman and other researchers are right in saying that "those born before cast a long shadow." It's interesting that Leman, himself a last-born, uses the word "shadow" rather than "beam," which, in some cases, it may be. There is a great need for a study focusing on the influence of siblings on each other, especially in large families in which older siblings help to care for the younger (and the younger get to wear the "hand-me-downs"). So many of Leman's traits for last-borns don't seem to fit in my case. For example, "charming, likable, fun to be with, people oriented, affectionate and engaging, caring, lovable, wanting to help, likes to get strokes and give them, entertaining and funny, knows how to get noticed"? That's not how I think of myself. On the other hand, as noted earlier, I identify with these descriptions: "Last borns are on a seesaw of emotions and experiences they find hard to explain or understand." I suppose one of the other five should be writing about the last-born. "Last borns are used to being put down or written off." "It's no wonder the last born grows up with an 'I'll show them' attitude." "Last borns 'just do it.'" I do recall thinking, "Ok, just wait. I'll show you—when I become a renowned chaplain in the Marines, or when I become a famous country/western singer, or when I become a world-famous evangelist like Billy Graham, or when I get four or five college degrees and write books." I saved up my money and bought a guitar from Sears, but never really learned to play (and sold it to a friend of Carolyn's at Moody). Blessed with a good memory, I was asked to "speak pieces" at Christmastime (not only at Sage School but at Berreman, Pleasant Valley, and Center Hill). I even tried writing early, sending some pieces to *Reader's*

Digest and even entered a sermon contest sponsored by *The Sword of the Lord*. I remember loving books at an early age and whenever I was asked what I wanted for Christmas, it was ordinarily a book, especially "a Jesus book," as I called them. I remember being fascinated with some comic book stories of classic novels (*The Three Musketeers, Moby Dick, Adventures of Huckleberry Finn* and *Tom Sawyer, The Hunchback of Notre Dame, Gulliver's Travels, The Corsican Brothers*, identifying with the Corsican brother and his "book-filled bedroom").

As a little kid, I played alone much of the time. I recall asking Mother once, at what age I don't remember (probably seven or eight), if she thought I was too big to play in the dirt with little cars and trucks. As always, she was so understanding in her response: "If you enjoy doing that, why not?" I built a shack down across from the ditch, constructed of old boards I found lying around, where I went for privacy, alone with my thoughts and imaginary friends I talked to, one of whom was "Mr. Krottely" (I *think* that's the way he spelled it). I never had many friends growing up—mainly Lester (Kantlehner), Bobby and Lloyd Nowak, later Bob and Dean Dixon.

As I think of growing up on the farm, I'm constantly amazed at the sovereign grace of God, in sustaining each of us. Word has it that the summer before I was born was a terribly hot one, and many wondered how Mother endured it. We all experienced the common childhood illnesses (whooping cough, chicken pox, measles, later mumps—and escaping the dreaded infantile paralysis or polio) and the brushes with serious accidents and death. There's the story of the hard cider and the girls getting into it in the cellar with the kerosene incubators nearby, when I was about three or four and everyone else was out working in the field (see Chapter IV, "Remembrance of Things Past: Sibling Dialogue"). There was also the time a huge iron fell off a shelf on the porch—onto my foot. And the time when Mel, Maynard, and John were swimming in Plum River—and I was wading around (not able to swim), when all of a sudden I stepped into a deep area of the river—and came close to drowning before Mel pulled me out. Or the time at Maynard's when we were putting bales of hay into the barn with the elevator. I was sitting on the tractor seat, but, for some reason, got off, only to see the elevator wheels sink into the soft mud and topple the elevator over right onto the tractor and across the seat where I had been sitting. Or the time Butch the dog and I were out in the middle of the sink-hole field, when the entire herd of cows, led by the bull, started chasing the dog, who ran to me for protection. Fortunately, we were able to outrun them and make it to the safety of the fence.

I guess I was a pretty serious-minded kid and thought a lot about death. One of my earliest memories is attending the funeral of Dad's Uncle Ed with my folks, sitting in that little country church and hearing the mournful, somber strains of the piano: plung-plaplung, plung-plaplung. Later when a distant cousin LeMoyne Kehl, who was about my age, passed away suddenly, I was struck by how uncertain and transient life is, that even a young person my age could die. Also a favorite Sunday School teacher, Jane Denier, a young woman in her twenties, died suddenly. Some time later, a neighboring farmer, Roy Mader, died suddenly when the hay poles, used for stacking hay, came loose and toppled over, striking and killing him instantly. At another time, a speeding car failed to negotiate a curve and struck a couple, the Frank Warfields, sitting in their yard at their place in the little village of Argo Fay, south of town. Then, too, I heard the news of how a little girl in Chicago (I even remember her name--Susanne Degnan) was murdered when someone broke into the home at night. All of these events compounded, and I became almost paranoid, worrying about dying, reluctant to go to sleep at night, afraid I might not wake up. How does a little kid handle that kind of phobia? Do you say to a parent or sibling or friend, "Hey, you know, I have this problem of worrying about death. Any suggestions?" Or does a seven- or eight-year-old say to the pastor, "Could I make an appointment with you to discuss my fear of death?" I did take some action, like warding off possible murderous break-ins by placing cans of rocks and metal on top of the bedroom's window ledges so when someone attempted to open them, it would awaken me. I was also careful not to lie on my back with hands folded across my chest, corpse-like, and took to sleeping only on my stomach. ("How did you like your browneyed boy, Mister Death?" e. e. cummings). Reader, you're probably thinking, "What a weird little kid"? Right. I lived with that phobia for years until it was alleviated by my faith in the Lord Jesus, Who conquered death (see more on Christian Faith in Chapter VIII), and by literature (such as Edward Taylor's "A Fig for Thee, O Death").

After graduating from high school in 1953 (see Chapter VI, "Telling Tales Out of School"), I enrolled in Bob Jones University as a ministerial student, earning a double major in Biblical Studies and English, working during the summer first for Dr. Mershon on the Palmer place, then painting with Bob Davis, later working at the Green Giant Canning Factory in Lanark. After graduation, I worked during the summer at a bank in downtown Buffalo, N.Y., then attended the University of Wisconsin, Madison, for a Master's Degree in English and Education, then taught English at the Roosevelt School, a private prep school in Stamford, Connecticut, and took graduate courses at Fordham University in the Bronx. The following summer I worked with a painting contractor in Philadelphia and took a night course at the University of Pennsylvania. The following year I taught in Pasadena, CA., substituting at Pasadena High School and taking courses at Occidental College and the University of Southern California. I worked evenings at World Vision in Pasadena, where a friend introduced me to Wanda Thomas. I agreed to sit with her at her friend's appearance in *The Messiah*, after which we began dating (first date: a play "Five Finger Exercise" at the Pasadena Playhouse). Wanda and I were married in Auburn, California, on August 10, 1963, moved to Arizona in 1965, where I began my career as Assistant Professor of English at Arizona State University in Tempe. I got the position without a personal interview, and Wanda got her job teaching 2nd grade at Monterey Park Elementary School in Phoenix, also without a personal interview, something unheard of then or now. We're thankful for two wonderful sons—Kevin and Kenyon—,two wonderful daughters-in-law—Kathie and Josette—, and five wonderful grandchildren—Emily, Aidan, and Owen, Bennett and Brynn.

Del & Wife Wanda

Del & Family (Wanda; Kevin, Kathie, Bennett, Brynn;
Kenyon, Josette, Emily, Aidan, Owen)

Much more could be said about the six of us. Concerning the siblings, Mary has said, "Since we never went away much, we spent long days working together and just hanging out. Many times after the work was done we were too tired for much else. Remember those *hot* (and humid) summers with no air-conditioning or even fans? Each sibling had an important place in my life, and I guess I wouldn't change much even though at times it was hard. We learned to do without and as Carolyn once said, 'We were poor, but we didn't know it.' As a whole, I *know* we had a better life than a lot of kids do today. Money isn't everything. We had enough (good) food, shelter, and more love than many others. All in all, I'd say life was pretty good to us." That's certainly a valid summary. God has poured out many blessings upon this family!

Look at the snapshot of the six of us, dressed in our Sunday finery, standing out in the yard (within sight of the "tree-trees" on the right), probably in 1941 or 42, the handsome older boys in fact casting a shadow to the right.

The six Kehl siblings on a Sunday morning, dressed for church

The four Kehl boys dressed for church

(Oh how I hated those short pants—and stockings no less!) Now look at us about fifty-three years later, also in the yard, John and the girls sitting, the other three guys standing behind, all of us bespectacled. And then note the snapshot of the six of us standing in the kitchen, in May of 2004, about six months before John's death.

The six Kehl siblings at the farm for a rare visit together

The six Kehl siblings together in the farmhouse

It's interesting to contemplate the life of each of us in this particular family, why God in His divine sovereignty gave us these parents and these particular siblings. In her novel *Emma*, Jane Austen wrote, "Nobody who has not been in the interior of a family can say what the difficulties of any individual of that family may be." Each of us, the six Kehl siblings, have had certain difficulties to face and know something of what the others have faced, but through the grace of God and the loving care of our parents and each other, we have been able to confront and surmount them. One of the figures in Robert Frost's "Death of the Hired Man" says, "'Home is the place where, when you have to go there, / They have to take you in,'" but another figure responds, "'I should have called it / Something you somehow haven't to deserve.'" We didn't have to "deserve" the loving, caring home we had—and besides, grace operates not on deserving or earning but on free giving—but surely each of the six siblings contributed much that is significant in making the Kehl household the happy home it was.

IV. Remembrance of Things Past: A Kehl Sibling Dialogue

"This is the happiest conversation, where there is no competition, no vanity, but a calm quiet interchange of sentiments."
  (Samuel Johnson, in Boswell's *Life of Samuel Johnson*)

"A single conversation across the table with a wise man is better than ten years' study of books."
  (Chinese saying, in H. W. Longfellow's *Hyperion*)

"Praising what is lost
Makes remembrance dear."
  (Shakespeare, *Twelfth Night*)

"'The time has come,' the Walrus said,
'To talk of many things:
Of shoes—and ships—and sealing wax—
Of cabbages—and kings.'"
  (Lewis Carroll, *The Walrus and the Carpenter*)

"Some little talk awhile of Me and Thee
There was."
  (Edward Fitzgerald, *The Rubaiyat of Omar Khayyam*)

One evening in May of 2004, the six Kehl siblings sat around the table in the kitchen at the farm, flanked by wives and members of their families, and spent about three hours reminiscing and sharing stories about our memories of growing up. It was a special time, one of the few times the six of us sat and remembered together—and the last the six siblings were together before John's homegoing six months later.

Del: Let's start with the eldest. Mel, what do you remember?

Mel: What do you want me to remember?

Del: I don't know; I can't tell you what to remember.

Mel: Well, we had a good time. My dad put me on a tractor when I was about eleven years old and we had a hired man that couldn't handle it, so Dad put me on, and the first ravine I came to I plowed across and after that I did good. Dad bought another tractor and we did real good. He bought a Fordson from Roy Spear. The blacktop was gravel then, and I drove that thing home from up there and got along fine, but you know when he bought that F-12 the wheels were tied together on it and I came to a little ditch and it rolled over on its side. He said, "Don't you tell Mother about that." (Laughter). He backed around with the Model A and we hooked onto it and set it back up and I drove it home the rest of the way. We put the cultivator on it the next day and cultivated corn with it. Ok?

Del: Yeah, that's good. You're next, Maynard. What do you remember most about growing up?

Louder. (Laughter)

Maynard: Well, we had a good time.

Del: Anything special stand out in your mind?

Maynard: Johnny and I always were together with everything. Played together. Trapped together. Beat the brush piles and shot the rabbits when they came out.

Del: And checked your traps every day before school?

Maynard: Um-humm. I remember I had traps down there across from Montaignes. Walked clear down there to look for them before I went to school.

Del: Sometimes ran into skunks and had problems when you went to school?

Mel: No, but every time we caught a fox those Randecker girls would say, "Those Kehl guys got another skunk." They couldn't tell the difference between a fox and a skunk. (Laughter)

Remember when Wilma always used to say, "As soon as Mel Kehl is on the school ground there's a fight," and the teacher said, "Yeah, and I notice the fight never starts till you get here." (Laughter).

Del: John?

John: Yes?

Del: What do you remember most about growing up with this crew?

John: Oh, I guess I had a good growing up time. Bad times and good times. I didn't like school. It was more fun to skin a cow, wasn't it, Maynard? Remember when we did that? We were late and Mother made us go to school anyway. Maynard and I did a lot of things together. We planted potatoes and sold 'em, and we just had a good time.

Del: And raised some peanuts?

John: Raised some peanuts.

Del: Who invented the peanut sheller? Was that you?

Maynard: Probably.

Del: You had your hand in that too, though?

John: Yeah, Yeah, Yeah.

Picture taken.

Del: Anything else?

John: I don't think so.

Mel: Remember that little bomb we made in the shop, and we set it off and ran out, and it knocked the windows out. (Laughter) Dad was a little upset about that. You know they always said you could never shock a chicken because they have feathers but we were playing with a magneto one time and I said to Maynard, "Stick that up under that rooster's wing." He was our tame rooster. And so I gave the magneto a flip, and when it got on his skin he got a shock and he went right out through the window too. (Laughter)

Del: Want to tell us what you did to the dogs with the turpentine? (Laughter) No, ok, let's move to the female side of the family now.

Carolyn: Well, I remember that John and I used to do everything together. I used to go crow shooting with him, and I remember one time we set traps. He was trapping for fox, and he had felt shoes on and I didn't. I froze my feet. So he says, "We have to look at the traps early in the morning." Well, the next morning he was sick, and he says, "You have to do it because you're the only one who knows where they are." So I ran back there, and he had a fox in, and it was pitch-dark yet; it was 4 o'clock. And so I came back home and got Dad and he went and got the fox.

Del: Ok, Mary. Want to tell us about when you climbed the windmill? (Laughter)

Mel and Carolyn: She probably doesn't remember.

Mary: I don't remember climbing the windmill, but I remember them telling about it, about Mel going to the window and Mother didn't know where I was, and he was laughing. (Laughter) Dad went out the next day and sawed the ladder off down to the ground so it wouldn't happen again.

John: I'll tell you how the windmill went down. The wheel got bad, and Dad said, "You ought to take that wheel off of there," and so I went up and I don't know how many spokes it had coming down to the hub, and I took all the nuts off, tied a rope on the wheel and hooked it on the tractor and gave it a jerk, and I got the wheel, tower, and all—and my rope wasn't any too long.

Several: Mary, you didn't tell your story.

Mel and Carolyn: She doesn't want us to know.

Del: What are you hiding from us? (Laughter)

Mary: Not a lot. I remember ... Do you remember the time I baked the cake, and Carolyn was supposed to be reading the recipe because I couldn't read yet? And I beat the egg whites and we forgot to put them in, and the cake raised up nice and then it went flat. I think they were doing potatoes out here. Remember that? We took the cake out and they ate it; we didn't frost it or anything; they just ate it.

John: Tell about the time Maynard had sand on his feet. (Laughter)

Del: You want to tell about it, Maynard?

Maynard: I guess we dug a hole and put sand in a 6 gallon crock. I don't know why I got down in the hole and put the crock down on my toes, then I couldn't get it out of there. Johnny ran down to the basement where they were sprouting potatoes and said, "Maynard's got sand on his feet." (Laughter) I guess they couldn't figure out what the deal was. Pretty soon Dad came down and lifted the crock off. (Laughter)

Mary: And it's still buried down there.

Del: Oh, it is?

John: I think it is.

Carolyn: What they did, they dug a hole the same size as the crock and then to lift it in there he got in the hole and lifted it in and then it was on his feet and he couldn't get out. (Laughter)

John: That was a smart thing to do, wasn't it?

Carolyn: So when John says, "Oh, Maynard's got sand on his feet," nobody paid any attention.

So what? So what? "You better come on; you better hurry up! Hurry up! He's got sand on his feet!" (Laughter)

Mel: Never wore shoes in the summertime anyhow.

Maynard: Pretty heavy on the ... (Laughter)

Del: Anything else on that?

John: We haven't heard much from you ...

Del: Well, I'm sorta moderating. Well, the most scary thing, I think, was when I was in 1st grade and Mother got ill. I don't know what it was, and I didn't know what was going on, but somebody came down to tell the teacher. I don't know who that was either. You can help fill in here ... Nobody bothered to say anything to me and I was sitting there wondering ... Or you either [Mary], I guess. The older kids, I guess, you [Carolyn] and John, went home...

John: I wasn't in school then.

Del: You weren't in school then. Ok.

Carolyn: That's not it at all.

Del: That's why you're here—to tell us what it was...

Carolyn: That's pretty emotional for me, and I'm not sure I want to tell that story ...

Del: Well, anyway, it's emotional for me too, because nobody told me what was going on and I knew something terrible had happened and so we had to wait till the end of school and come home and find out that Mother was gravely ill and almost had died, I guess ...

Carolyn: Nah.

Del: No? Ok, well, you set us straight then since you know …

Carolyn: I don't want to tell the whole story …

Del: Ok, we can go on to something else then …

Carolyn: I do want to say that she had a gall bladder attack and she thought she was going to die. I'm sure anybody who has ever had that thinks they are. Dad and the boys were up in Loran—wasn't it Loran?—tearing down a house. I had to stay home from school because she wasn't feeling well and she needed a doctor, and she sent me to school. And she had Floyd Howard go home and call them and call the doctor. But .

Mary: Of course, we didn't have a telephone; that's why …

Carolyn: We had no telephone.

Del: Well, the thing that stands out in my mind as I look back over our life together is the grace of God. You know, we're sitting around this table—six of us. We're all still living; we all have our faculties …

John: We do? (Laughter)

Del: Well, in a manner of speaking … (Laughter)
But I praise the Lord for how good He was to our family, and we could each of us, I think, specify close calls we've had—not only our parents but our close calls with death, and God has spared us—for a purpose, and I'm thankful for that, and I'm thankful that He's allowed the six of us to sit here together and have this reunion—and all of you *there*—and we appreciate all of you and love all of you. Anyway, I just wanted to say that in praise to the grace of God for sparing us through these years. And how our parents were able to hang onto this farm during the Depression. We were talking when we came through Woodbine today about riding up there to make payments on the farm and how God enabled Mother through her chickens and egg money to keep us really, I think, going with clothes … And I just want to praise the Lord for His grace and the fact

that they were able to hang onto the farm through thick and thin. So those are my thoughts initially.

Mel: I remember when they bought that farm. You know, I was old enough to remember all that. We spent a lot of time in at the bank and a couple of the aunts in Rockford wanted big bucks, you know. "That farm's worth a lot of money." So, anyhow, after about three or four times in there Ralph Eaton, Dad's lawyer, got ahold of them and said, "I tell you what, what's gonna happen: if you keep this up, Harry's just gonna move off that farm and you guys can have it. If you want to go home and say, 'Well, we're going to the home place,' fine, but you'd better sign off, because the way times are, he's not gonna pay any more money. He can go and get another farm somewhere else. It's that simple." So I guess they thought about it a little bit and they finally decided that they'd do that. But anyhow, if it hadn't been for Ralph Eaton, they probably would have balked ... I think their husbands were telling them, "Hey, you get a lot more money than that, get a lot more money than that." But it was a tough time and, you know, they had a tough go till the war came along and everything picked up. When the war came along, everybody was making money ... Everybody but me ... (Laughter)

Mary: And to add to that, I'd like to thank Dad for selling the farm to Johnny so we can still come.

Several: Yeah. Right.

Del: John and I were talking this afternoon about a time I don't remember because I was too small but thanking the Lord for how He worked through our mother, for us to come to Christ, to know about the plan of Salvation and how through reading *The Sword of the Lord* and hearing "The Old Fashioned Revival Hour" on the Moody radio station she came to understand the gospel—that you need to come to Christ. I don't remember the time when the whole family knelt around the radio ... Would some of you tell about that? John?

John: I remember it very well. And it meant something to me. And I think, you know, it was real. But then in later years I dedicated my life to the Lord again, and I've lived for Him ever since, and I'm not sorry ...

Del: Amen! Anybody else remember that time? I don't; I've only heard tell about it.

Carolyn: Yeah, I remember it. It was, I believe, a Sunday night and it was Charles E. Fuller, I think.

Mary: Right.

Carolyn: And she gave the invitation here, for all of us.

Del: And you all knelt and prayed?

Carolyn: Um-hum.

Del: Do you remember that, Mary?

Mary: I sure do!

Carolyn: I don't know if you [Mel] were here. Were you?

Mel: Yeah.

Mary: And, of course, her reading *The Sword of the Lord,* knowing the Rices, when the evangelistic services came to Mt. Carroll, that's how we got going and how we got started at the Church of God. And how Johnny met Agnes.

Mel: I can tell you why she went to the Church of God. I remember when, you know, Dad's folks all went to the Methodist Church. Mom was raised Lutheran in Massbach. During the Depression, she said, "I go to church because of what I believe; I don't go there to see how much I can dress up," and some of these deep thinkers would come in all dressed up real neat, and she said, "I don't need that." That's when they started going to the Church of God. I remember when she started going there. I remember that very, very clearly.

Mary: Do you remember her talking about when she went to German Reformed school, the year she took off school? Was it her and Rudy that went for Confirmation at the Lutheran Church in German? Do you remember her telling about that?

Carolyn: Well, they did that in the wintertime. They actually went to the church and had school and the instruction for Confirmation; it was all in German.

Mary: But she told me they never once mentioned Salvation. It was only after she got away from that that she heard about Salvation.

Carolyn: Yeah.

Del: Maybe we can concentrate on just what we remember about our parents, what we remember about Mother and Dad. I'll start off by saying that I really appreciated both of them. Dad, you know, was very moody at times. We were talking today about some of the things … Sometimes he'd get angry and he wouldn't speak to anybody for a while and we'd say, "I wonder what's bothering him." Well, we'd have to wait a few days and finally it would come out. He was a hard worker. He was a good man. Wouldn't work on Sunday, etc. And Mother was such a devout, godly woman who prayed daily for us, and we're so thankful for that. I'm so thankful for her. Who wants to share what you remember about Mother and Dad?

Mel: The thing I remember, you know, I worked with Dad probably more than the rest of the boys did, but I never had any problems with Dad. He and I always got along great. The only time that I remember that I really got upset with him, we were sorting hogs down here and Mom was out there. It was sloppy out there; it was in the spring and it was muddy and everything. And one of the hogs got by and he just read the riot act to her and, you know, he had been in a bad mood and been growling and I said, "Well, you tell us which one you want and we'll get em in there; just don't be giving her heck." You know, and she looked at me so funny. You know, I guess she couldn't believe that I had talked … and that's the only time I ever talked back to him, but it just hit me wrong and I guess maybe the German in me came out [Laughter] because it really teed me off, I'll tell you, and I guess maybe… he tamed down then and he was real great all the rest of the day. But it was the only time I ever talked back to him.

Del: Carolyn, want to share?

Carolyn: I, I think I thought he was perfect. I think there was a time when I decided that he wasn't and I was really disappointed. And I used to, I used to love to sit on his lap when I was little. I used to love to sit on his lap and listen to his watch, his pocket watch, but I, you know, I guess I really thought he was something.

Del: You were always "Bape."

Carolyn: I was Bape.

Del: You were "Carleger" to the rest of us. (Laughter)

Mel: You were kinda his chosen one.

Mary: Yeah, that's what I was gonna say. I didn't have any problem with Dad, but I knew I wasn't his little girl. But I spent a lot of time with Mother. I guess I spent more time with her than probably anybody else.

Maynard: I know Mother was more tolerant and easy-going than he was. Get away with more. Up to a point...

Del: I remember when you were dating the Dinderman girl and he would want to know where you were going—remember?—and I remember one time you took off up toward Maders to sort of fool him. (Laughter) So he wouldn't know where you were going. Was that true?

Maynard: That's true. (Laughter)

Mel: You know, that was really weird ... When I came back from the service, I think it was John ... I was sitting here, you know, and he came downstairs, and Dad said, "Where you going?" and John said, "Out"—and out the door he went and slammed the door behind him. (Laughter) Boy, I never got by with that stuff when I was going out. (Laughter) I always had to get approval.

John: Every Saturday night Maynard would ask Dad, "Can I go away?" "Well, yeah, if you get up in the morning." It was always a weekly thing, but he never got up in the morning. (Laughter)

John: Well, I love my Dad very much, and I was with him almost all the time, and I got along well with him until I got old enough to run around and then we didn't hit it off very well. He always wanted to know where I was going and I didn't always know where I was going so he'd be mad at me either way, so I just, I just didn't talk about it.

Mel: You just said you're going out. (Laughter)

John: "Well, what if something happens and we come to look for you?" "I don't know." I guess I was kind of ornery in some ways, but I'd tell Mother; if Mother wanted to know I'd tell Mother. I got along well with my Mother, and I still miss my Mother, after all these years ...

Del: We all do...

John: I'm sorry...

Del: That's ok. It's nothing to be ashamed of. We all miss Mother—and Dad too.

John: Yup.

Del: I think the thing I remember, vividly, about my Dad was one Sunday afternoon he always took a nap. They both did. But he took a nap and he was sleeping and I thought a nice thing to do would be to go out and pound the nails in the siding of the house. (Laughter) I thought this would be a very helpful thing to do, so I went outside and I started pounding nails and I thought, "Oh boy, this is good; I'm being good." (Laughter) And he came out there and grabbed a rubber tube and laid it on. (Laughter) I remember that licking very vividly. And I decided ... I was really upset. I was gonna run away from home. (Laughter). But then I knew I'd have to miss dinner [laughter], so I didn't run away from home but I was really unhappy about getting that spanking, which I deserved, I must admit ... (Laughter) Probably should have had more ...

Mel: Did you ever get paddled with a piece of bead off the old Model-T tire?

Del: I don't think so. I don't remember that. Is that what you got?

Mel: Mom had that up on the high-shelf on the stove. I never did get beat with it, but it was a good deterrent. (Laughter)

John: He had that razor strap too.

Carolyn and Others: Yeah, he always had that razor strap. The razor strap was hanging on the wall there, and he threatened with it.

Del: That was a major deterrent, right?

Carolyn: Well, I think I got the whippin' when we broke the eggs.

Mary: I don't remember getting a lickin' but I remember breaking the eggs.

Carolyn: Oh, no, I don't think you got it. I got it. (Laughter)

Del: What's the story of breaking the eggs?

Carolyn: Well, we went in the chicken house and the chicken house had a door to the hog house, and we took the eggs and we threw 'em against the hog house and it was really fun watching them run down. (Laughter) And she came out to gather the eggs, and she couldn't figure out why there weren't any eggs, until she got to the door, and she saw where the eggs went. And I ran. I was good at running. (Laughter) Dad had the old Fordson, with the double wheels on, in the corncrib and there was only about that much space between the wheel and the wall. I got in the wheel. She could not get me. But she waited till I came out.

Del: And then you got it.

Carolyn: Then I got it.

Del: What did you get, Mary?

Mary: I don't remember gettin' anything.... .

Carolyn: Mary got it when we did the comb case ...

Mary: Yeah, when we were down at ... Who lived down ... ?

Carolyn: Nobles.

Mary: When Nobles lived down there, Mother was down there helping cook for threshers or whatever. And she took us along and ...

Carolyn: Mary Herring ...

Mary: Old Mary Herring was there ... (Laughter)

Carolyn: Yeah, what they did, they set out the wash basin and the water and the ...

Del: It's called a scob ...

Carolyn: What?

Del: Scob. I'm sorry, go ahead ... (Laughter)

Carolyn: They set out the wash basin and the towel and all that for the men to wash up before they came in for dinner, and they had a comb case that was hanging up high, and I wanted to see what was in it, so, of course, it was tin and I knocked it down. And she came flying out of the door—Aunt Mary Herring—she came flying out of the door, and I just ran and jumped off the porch, and Mary got it. (Laughter)

Mary: The woman should have known I couldn't reach it. (Laughter)

John: Who'd we shivaree the time we set the Thunderbolt in that old stove?

Maynard: Ruth, I guess. Pooey.

John: Blew a hole in the wall.

Maynard: Warming oven, and we put the Thunderbolt in there and shut the door. (Laughter) I guess the smoke came out inside the house. (Laughter) We still didn't get 'em outa the house, though, did we? Never got anything out of 'em.

Del: Those shivarees were something, weren't they?

John: Um-humm.

Del: Too bad they discontinued them.

John: Did they discontinue them?

Del: Haven't they?

John: They shivareed Edna and me.

Del: Oh, did they really? Did you have an ice-cream supper then?

John: No, they had stuff in the church. We all went in there then. But you should have seen ... I had done something to somebody's bicycle and I was just coming down and I saw that row of cars coming up, and I knew what was happening. (Laughter) She said, "What'll we do?" I said, "Well, you better get in the house and change your clothes." (Laughter)

Del: So that's the end of the story?

John: That was the surprise. Yeah.

Del: Well, we could share what we remember about each other now, I guess. There's a certain goat story that we might want to talk about. (Laughter) Remember the goats? Goats?

Mary: Were you [Mel] here when the goats were here?

Del: I guess you were gone...

Mary: Maynard remembers...

Del: He remembers the goat story, since he's the … . He had a major part in it…

Maynard: Yeah, they got up on my Model-A and tramped a hole through the top. I threw a stove wood stick at em and broke one's leg…

Del: Um-humm, and didn't tell anybody …

Maynard: I didn't tell anybody. (Laughter)

Del: The word was that the goat had crawled up on something and broken its own leg.

(Laughter)

Mel: If it wouldn't have crawled up, it probably wouldn't have got its leg broke. (Laughter)

Del: Yeah. Goats do crawl though; they climb. Anyway, we liked the goats. And Carolyn milked the goat…

Mary: And fed it to the cats…

Carolyn: Well, Dad liked it.

Del: We had one chained in the old hog house next to the window; the window was open, and we went out; I think we went to church or somewhere and came home and somebody looked back there and saw the goat hanging out the window. It had jumped out and was hanging there …

John: Committed suicide … That was a good …

Mary: Yeah, the boys didn't care about that …

Del: Well, so much for the goat story … Now we move on to other things. (Laughter)

Mel: Remember our pet pigeon, how it used to sneak in the house and peck the girls on the toe when they were standing by the stove? Remember that?

Mary: I remember your squirrel …

Mel: Remember that pet pigeon we had …

Several: The squirrel … And the crow …

Mary: I had a long, a great big long pencil up on top of the glass cupboard, and your squirrel climbed up there and chewed it up.

Mel: I had those three gray squirrels that time, and it was snowing and drifting the thing shut where I kept them so I brought them in and they were in the little closet back here on the clothes, and I came in and said, "Where's my squirrels?" And Mom said, "I don't know where those stupid things are." Anyhow, I looked for them and I couldn't find them. She had a box where she had sox that she was patching and she reached down in there and she let out a scream and said, "There's your stinking squirrel." (Laughter)

Del: Yeah, remember the crow?

Mel: Yeah, Dad used to put a pancake in his pocket and that crow would land on his shoulder and go down there and take that pancake out.

Del: Remember the time you had the old puddle-jumper and you drove down to—who was it who lived down there?—Nowak or was it Potter? Anyway, and the crow jumped out from down below …

John: I know I drove down to Maynards one time with the truck, and the crow stuck his head out from under the truck and started hollering and carrying on.

Del: Maybe that's the same story …

John: Probably is.

Del: Anything else about the crow, the squirrel, the pigeon?

Maynard: Yeah, that crow rode down underneath the truck, hopped around down there, and when we got ready to go home, he didn't like to be handled too much. Johnny caught him and brought him back home.

John: How about the time your truck took off and [???unintelligible] realize it was his truck? (Laughter)

Maynard: Water ran down the shiftin lever in the transmission and froze… I jacked the back wheel up and left it run a little while. I had to go over to Potters and help him cut wood. I told Bernice to shut that off after while. She looked down there and she said the truck was gone and she saw the dog looking down over the river bank. (Laughter) It ran clear across there and through the fence, clear down to the river. Muffler was lying up on the bank.

Del: Anybody want to share about the old buggy that you used to ride down the hill?

Mel: Dad pulled that old buggy out of the shed back there, and we took everything off of it but the box and the wheels and the axle, and we had it fixed with a chain that went to the front axle and had it fastened to the box and you could steer it that way. John never trusted getting in it. Right? He always stuck a plank onto the box and over the back. I wasn't with them that day, but it was Halloween and they had a whole load of pumpkins on the thing. They went down the hill and it'd go halfway up that other hill over there. And some way or other that chain broke and Johnny jumped off. And he was the only one who got hurt. I guess the Frederick kids were on there too, weren't they?

John: Harvey was.

Mel: Anyhow, the thing rolled over and dumped all the pumpkins out, and John jumped off and on that gravel over there, that flint rock, he got scratched up a little bit. Mom says, "That's enough of that stuff. You aren't going to take that to school any more."

Del: Oh, you used to take it to school?

Mel: Yeah. That's where they were headed—to school.

Carolyn: Didn't you take the cousins down the road here, that one time?

John: I think the day before that, the cousins were here.

Carolyn: Marilyn and Darlin and Donna Jean and all them. Remember that?

Mel: Yeah.

Carolyn: Took em down this way …

Mel: That thing would really go.

Maynard: No brakes on it.

John: No brakes on it.

Mel: No way to stop it. (Laughter)

Del: I thought you made a brake for it.

Mel: No, we never had brakes on it.

John: We never got that far … We wanted to go, didn't want to stop. (Laughter)

Carolyn: Just run up the next hill to stop …

Del: It was fun going on sleds down there too, wasn't it?

Mel: That one year when we had all that ice, that was really something … .

Carolyn: Oh, yeah.

Mel: Go down that hill so fast. It was unbelievable how fast we went down that hill.

Maynard: Sometimes we'd go down there crossways.

Del: You always hoped you didn't meet a car coming…

Mel: You didn't meet many cars with all that ice … .

John: Not much traffic on that road … .

Maynard: No, you didn't see many cars out on that road.

Mel: That morning after that rain, Dad said, "I better go out and shut those hogs in," and the hogs were underneath the hog house, you know, in that basement thing there, and I remember him walking out there, and there was a gate lying there on its side, and he made the mistake of stepping on that gate. Course, it had ice on it and what it did, it cracked and made a noise, and those pigs went oof, oof, oof—and down the hill they went into that ditch down there. We spent almost all day getting them back up there, didn't we? You talk about a hog on ice, that's no kiddin! (Laughter)

Mary: Speaking about ice, Del and I mentioned the other day about the time Johnny took us to school in the old Model-A, and it was so icy we had trouble, and I think Del said somebody even bumped into the back of us … .

John: I didn't have the Model-A then. I had my [??] then …

Mary: Well, anyhow, we struggled all the way in to school, and when we got there, there wasn't any school.

John: There wasn't any school?… I didn't remember that …

Del: Remember the winter it snowed so much and blew and the road was totally drifted shut and then it froze and you were driving over the top of it?

John: Driving over the top of it, yeah … I remember coming down the hill over here by Wolf's, I wanted to play around a little bit and I got off to the side and it was … brush there and it was hollow under there and I broke through. Marv and his dad came walking by and picked it up and lifted it out of there. (Laughter)

Carolyn: Well, I remember that storm. I was a freshman in high school. Dad picked me up and we had to shovel to get around this corner down here on this hill before we could get home. I missed a week of school, and I was upset about that. Yes, I was upset about missing a week of school.

Del: We used to pray for snow days.

Carolyn: Not me.

Del: Anybody else want to share anything about growing up? Each other?

Mary: I thought about when we came up the highway yesterday about the time the dog bit Dad?

John: Yeah, we went down there to help saw wood and I said we better take a gun. "Oh, no." Well, the stupid dog bit him and I would've come home. Bit him right in the knee. I guess he was throwing wood and when he got done he couldn't walk. Judas brought him home.

Del: So what ever happened to the dog?

John: For some reason or other he died …

Del: … a premature death?

John: … by getting two bullets through him.

Del: Well, you want to tell us a little bit about that? What happened?

Mike: Why not? The dog's dead … (Laughter)

John: He never bit me, but he bit just about everybody else …

Mel: I guess he washed out down there …

Carolyn: Yeah.

John: Yeah. That was kinda stupid. I threw him in the crick and when they put the crick fence in that spring they found him. They weren't sure who shot him. They knew Judases had a big rifle; they knew we did. So they weren't sure.

Del: Mysterious disappearance, huh?

John: Yeah.

Mary: Poor guy's dead anyhow so it doesn't matter.

Mel: Yeah, he's been dead for quite a few years.

John: Better to be shot. He growled at me before I shot him though. (Laughter)

Maynard: Reason enough to shoot him.

Mary: Guess you shot him up, didn't you?

Carolyn: Maybe he was telling you not to do it.

John: One wasn't enough so I gave him another one. (Laughter)

Mel: Did you ever know about Mabel Randecker sticking her pencil in my arm?

Del: Oh yeah, I remember hearing about it.

John: I thought that was Wilma who did that.

Mel: Wilma, yeah.

Carolyn: Yeah, it was Wilma. I've never figured out why they called Alice "Bounce." Do you know, Maynard?

Maynard: I don't know.

Carolyn: They always called her "Bounce."

Del: Mabel's nickname was "Mushmouth."

Mel: She talked like she had a mouthful of mush. (Laughter) That's probably why she was called that.

John: Danny's was "Fiddlepants." (Laughter)

Carolyn: I was gonna' say, we weren't gonna' talk about that. (Laughter)

Jackie: Most of the gallery doesn't know how you got that "Carlager" name.

Mary: He nicknamed everybody, didn't you, Mel?

Mel: I, ah, well … She was in first grade, I think, and she was sitting right down below in the little seats down below me, and I was looking where she had signed her name and that's what it said. (Laughter)

Carolyn: Well, we didn't learn to print. We learned to write and that's what they said how I wrote my name.

Del: "Carlager" And this was Puss [Maynard]. Since we're talking about nicknames. Puss, right? How did that come about—Puss in Boots?

Mel: No, we used to watch Tom Mix and he had this … I don't remember how it was, but they had this Chinese cook, and he had this guy on there by the name of "Sneezy Snider" and he called him "Sneezy Puss," and he used to sneeze, so we started calling him "Puss."

Maynard: I'd get up in the morning and walked on the cold floor, I'd have to sneeze. I still do that.

Del: Still do that?

John: He'd blow his nose and hold his handkerchief [??]… (Laughter)

Mel: You talk about Tom Mix, we used to listen to Tom Mix and …

Carolyn: The Lone Ranger

Mel: Yeah, the Lone Ranger… Jack Armstrong. You know they each had a 15 minute program, but you only heard about 5 minutes of it. Each one of us had our chores to do and Maynard milked. That's all Maynard did was milk that cow. He'd get his coat and cap and overshoes on and get his milk bucket, and he'd sit down there and listen, and Mom'd say, "Go milk your cow." "Yeah, just as soon as this story's over." And then another one'd come on. "Go milk your cow." "As soon as this story's over." (Laughter) And it would be darker than it is right now and he still hadn't milked the cow. (Laughter)

John: Sitting there with his coat and cap and everything on, ready to go …

Mel: And his bucket in his hand. (Laughter)

John: Remember how Mary used to wipe her nose? (Laughter)

Mike: We need a word picture of that. (Laughter)

John: Like this … Remember that, Mary?

Carolyn (?): One more time, for the record.

Del: And this guy's [John] nickname was "Runt." Wasn't it?

John: Yup.

Del: I don't know what else. Were there other nicknames?

Mel: You know, the thing that I really remember about Dad … We were talking about Dad. We were going up across Plum River down there with the threshing machine and that Old Titan, and I guess he knew we were gonna get stuck in there … He had the Fordson down there, and he said, "Johnny, back that down here." Well, here comes the Runt down with the tractor …

John: I wasn't very old …

Mel: … and I thought Dad you should have known better than that, and it started rolling, and here's the Titan sitting there and Dad's behind it trying to hold it, and I thought, "Boy, I'm gonna' lose a brother and a dad right here in one easy operation." I'm standing there, and, you know, there was nothing I could do. I couldn't back up, and so he finally … What'd he do?

John: He grabbed the wheel and flipped it, and I backed into the river.

Mel: Yeah, you ran along the edge of the river but the back wheels were in the river. Boy, I was scared that time.

John: That tractor didn't have any brakes on it, and when you got on a hill, if you had it in reverse, you had to get it out of reverse and get it into forward gear. I just wasn't good enough at it, and I missed the gear and …

Mel: When you put it outa' gear, then you had nothing at all.

John: Yeah. That one Maynard drove had brakes on it. It would stop. I backed into a tree over in the timber one time that I missed the gear, and I hit that tree pretty hard. Good thing I hit the tree or I would have gone in the ditch.

Mel: You know he and I were hauling lumber, wood for the fire … This is one thing I think about every once in a while … And we had that old manure spreader; we took the box of it off, you know, and he's driving the tractor. The ground was froze, and you know we always just dropped a pin down through, never put a bolt or anything or nut on the bottom of it. And he's going down, after he got through the gate back there, going down through that … and he had that tractor in high, and it would run pretty fast, you know, and I'm sitting back there on the reach. That pin came out and that thing dug in the ground and those wheels just piled up, and that reach hit me up here, and the blood just running … It knocked me out for a minute … And he was gone; he was almost down to the timber, you know, and I get up, shake my head and look, and there he is going down there, and all of a sudden he looked back. And he was really upset; he thought it had knocked my eye out, you know, but the blood was running out right in my eyebrow; it really wiped a hole in there … He was scared that time …

Question from the Gallery (?): Wanda, we heard a story about a pet rooster...

Carolyn and Mel: Oh, you mean with the mouse?

Mel: You remember that?

Mary: Sort of, yeah.

Mel: I think that's when Delmar was born ...

Carolyn: Who was here? Who was here that time? Was that Baird and ...?

Mel: Yeah.

Carolyn: Clyde and ...?

John: Tony Kehl?

Maynard: Clyde.

Carolyn: Clyde ... That bunch from Rockford...

Mel: Yeah. But I think it was when he was born, wasn't it?

Carolyn: I don't remember that.

Mel: I think that might have been.

Del: So are you gonna' tell the story?

Mel: Yeah. We had this big old pet rooster and, you know, you'd catch a mouse and he'd eat the thing, so we tied a string on the mouse and the rooster swallowed the mouse and then we'd pull it back out again. (Laughter)

Carolyn: They did that till the rooster wouldn't swallow it any more. (Laughter)

John: Can you blame him? (Laughter)

Carolyn: No

Del: Then there's the story about the cats they put over the clothesline.

Mel: Oh, yeah. But we had a little electric fence control on this south window here, you know, and the cats used to sit on the outside there. Remember that? Your pet cats?

Carolyn: Yeah, my pet cats. Hear that, Terry, my pet cats? They were *my* cats.

Mel: We put this copper wire out there and we had this electric fence inside and those cats sat out there, and we'd wait till they got good asleep and we'd set that thing on, get it going, touch it down on those cats and their tails'd get that big around ... (Laughter) jump in the air ... The payoff was that time was Mom was coming up from the privy, and she saw those cats. Boy, she came through the door and she was not a happy camper! (Laughter)

John: I think probably the meanest thing you and I did, Maynard, was the time we tied the two cows' tails together and turned them out ... (Laughter)

Del: Two cows?

John: Two cows—we tied their tails together.

Del: Oh, I never heard that one before.

Mary: I never did either.

John: One of them had a tail, and the other one didn't. (Laughter)

Del: Oh my! The truth is really coming out tonight ...

Mary: Was it Johnny that shot an egg in the saucer?

John: Yeah, Carolyn was supposed to eat the egg and she must have tattled. (Laughter)

Maynard: My BB gun, and she hid the gun …

Carolyn: Yeah, that was the pump airgun, wasn't it?

John: Just a spring loader …

Carolyn: Yeah, and it was a tin saucer and it hit the saucer and made a dimple in it …

Mel: It had kind of a granite lining, and it had a real big dent in it. When Mom saw that she wasn't real happy …

Carolyn: Yeah, she wasn't happy … .

Maynard: I told her it was my gun and I said I didn't do it, and she said, "Well, I don't care …"

Mary: She didn't like guns anyway, did she?

Maynard: No, she didn't.

Carolyn: John's deal and my deal.

Del: And somebody had a little pet chicken and put it somewhere and she forgot where she put it …

Carolyn: Yeah, I did. We had these hens and they all had chickens and so one of them got lost and couldn't find the right hen, so I took it as a pet, brought it in the house. We were playing, and the shed out here had the corn planter, so we were playing so I thought, "Ok, I don't want the chick running around," so I put it in one of the planter boxes … Forgot all about it and next I couldn't find it. Looked all around, and I was really unhappy because couldn't find my chick. Mother said, "You can have any chick you want." So sometime during the next day I remembered where I put it—and it was ok. It was ok. Found it.

Del: So that story ends happily.

So do you want to share anything about wonderful Sage School. You [Mel] mentioned the pencil in your arm ... Anything else you remember about Sage, in particular?

Mel: Maybe I better tell the story on this ... I don't remember exactly how it happened... . Wilma walked up to sharpen her pencil, and she came back, and she had poked me or something when she went up, and coming back, I was gonna' get even with her, and she came at me with that pencil and she had just sharpened it and I put my arm up like this to keep from getting hit in the side of the head, and she stuck that in my arm and it broke it off way up in the wood. I dug the wood out myself. And I get home and Dad, when he found out about it, says, "Well, that's lead; you better get down ...—the road was blocked; we couldn't get out; the snow was blocking up the road—"and have Howard Schmidt take you to the doctor." Well, we went in to Doc Colehour. He says, "That's nothing but carbon; that won't hurt anything; I'm not gonna cut it out of there." It was in there for about a year and finally worked its way out. But, of course, the teacher parked her car down there and Howard had to tell her all about it the next morning, and when I walked into school that morning I knew that she knew ... . She was out in the coal shed, getting a bucket of coal, when it happened. She was not happy either. Gave us heck.

Maynard: ... I don't know what they did that time, do you?

Carolyn: Well, John, you know ... I never did know what they did, but you said ...

John: They put live shells in the furnace and stuff like that ... And they threatened to castrate Floyd Howard. (Laughter)

Maynard: I remember that. (Laughter) And she sent me out to get a switch then ... .

Carolyn: Yeah.

Maynard: ... to give them a lickin' ...

Mel: Well, he really wasn't the one to send after a switch ...

Carolyn: Why?

Mel: You know, there used to be a dog up by the post office that would run out and nip you in the leg every time you rode by. Remember that? And Maynard and I were in there and that dog came out there and I said, "You know, he grabs you by the leg every time he gets a chance"—'cause I'd slow up going through there—and he said, "Well, go down in the park and I'll get a switch." So we down there and he cut a willow switch and we came back up, and the dog came out—Yip, Yip, Yip, you know—and all of sudden the dog was quiet and I looked back and he was lying in the street there. I said to Maynard, I said, "Did you hit him?" and he said, "Yeah," and I said, "With that switch?" and he said, "Yeah, I used the big end." (Laughter) It just knocked him out. It must have hit him just right. (Laughter) He didn't chase motorcycles any more. (Laughter) Remember that one you ran over down there at the bottom of the big hill?

John: No, he didn't run out any more either.

Mel: Oh, man, he was bad. That was a German Shepherd, and you ran over it with the motorcycle ...

Del: Didn't you hit one with Dad on behind?

John: That was south of town, that one ...

Carolyn: That must have been quite a bump, if you hit a German Shepherd ...

Mel: Dorothy was with me that night, because my headlight wasn't working and so he said, "Well, you ride ahead of me and you can use my light," so I came down and I was just getting ready to go around the corner, and all of once here was his headlight up in the tops of the trees. (Laughter) He came up alongside of me and he says, "I ran over a dog," and I said, "No kiddin!" (Laughter)

John: Remember the time we came back from Clinton and it was pouring down rain, on the motorcycle?

Carolyn: Yup.

John: I dropped you off at the doctor and I think he thought you were crazy. (Laughter)

Carolyn: Yup, I got quite a few nice rides on the motorcycle.

Mel: Dad was the hot-rodder on that thing, wasn't he?

John: He liked to ride on the motorcycle…

Del: He loved it …

Mel: "Pass him! Pass him! Pass him!" (Laughter) Don't care how fast the car was going, "Pass him!"

??: What did you ever do with your old '39?

Mel: I traded it on that Indian that the guy pulled in front of me that I wrecked … . I hit him so hard that the doors on that old Plymouth flew open. (Laughter) No kiddin'

John: What did he do—pull out in front of you?

Mel: Made a left turn in front of me. I flew up over the top of the hood and I must have hit my head on the door and I jumped up and I said, "You old goat, where do you think you're going?" There were a couple old gals standing on the street, rubbing their hands like that … (Laughter)

Maynard: That was a good old motorcycle.

Mel: Yes, it was. Yeah.

What were you [Carolyn] gonna' tell now?

Carolyn: I think we've probably got it on there, but Danny Randecker and Wayne Schubert got a whipping. John says they put shells or blasting caps or something in the furnace, and the teacher sent Maynard out to cut a switch. She whipped 'em in front of the whole school …

Maynard: She whipped one a while and then she'd whip the other one a while.

Carolyn: Yup … and the switch that Maynard brought was green so some of the sap flew off and hit one of the little kids and so that one's crying …

Del: Was that Alma Schmidt?

Carolyn: Yup. That was the times when the teacher had control of the class. There was no BS-ing around.

Mel: You know, Jerry Schubert tells me about something that happened, and she was quizzing the kids down to find out—I don't know who the teacher was—she was quizzing the kids down to find out who had done whatever it was that they did, and she gets to Delmar and he says, "Teacher, I cannot tell a lie; Jerry Schubert did it." (Laughter)

Del: I don't remember that … (Laughter) That's what he said, huh?

Mel: That's what he said … (Laughter)

Del: I don't remember that one … But it's coming back … (Laughter)

Carolyn: Another school story on Del was …

Del: Oh, boy, here we go …

Carolyn: We'd start off for school and Del would have a stomach-ache …

Del: Yeah.

Carolyn: … so Mother would let him stay home. So she found out that after we went to school he was ok …

Del: Remarkable how much better I felt after everybody left … (Laughter)

Carolyn: So one day here comes Mother with Del—she brought him to school. School was already in session and so he was, I think, embarrassed …

Del: It was very embarrassing …

Carolyn: That didn't happen any more …

Del: No, it didn't happen any more … (Laughter). You're right. Exactly right.

That one I remember very well …

Carolyn: You remember that one?

John: Once you got him going, you couldn't keep him outa' school.

Mary: Yeah, he's still going…

Del: More or less…

Maynard: I didn't particularly like school. Try to get out of it any way I could.

Del: But you were good at it, weren't you?

Maynard: Well, I guess, when I decided to …

John: What I liked about school was when it was over … (Laughter) I didn't like school …

Del: Recess was your favorite?

John: Yeah. Recess … I wished in later years that I had applied myself, but I didn't think I needed it but if somebody had sat down with me and said, you know, how important this is … And I tried to do that with my kids—you know, get an education because it's important. And I wanted to stay home … I'd rather stay home and work than go to school, but you know, certain things have been hard for me. After Agnes died I had to learn how to write checks, keep the checkbook up and that stuff. And it came fairly easy for me. So, you know, if I had applied myself, some of those things would have been a lot easier for me. So get an education when you can …

Carolyn: One of the things that I remember is when we had Christmastime, have a social: everybody brought pies, cakes, cookies, fudge… We always had a Christmas program, the whole school. The whole neighborhood came, not just the families that had kids, and then they auctioned off the baked goods and we bought library books. And the same way with the end of school—the last day of school the whole neighborhood came for a picnic. It was something else to have the whole neighborhood, and they were working in the field. They'd stop and come and have dinner—lunch, whatever—and I remember Mother used to make … instead of baking bread, she'd make rolls, bigger than hamburger buns, and she'd put ham—and so they were ham sandwiches—and those were the first ones to go, because everybody knew that she had made those… That was a fun time.

Del: Yeah, it was—and those Christmas programs were a lot of work. We'd start practicing for those …

John: We put on some good plays…

Del: …weeks and weeks ahead of time.

Carolyn: And one time somebody donated a turkey, and they raffled the turkey and I think Dad bought, you know, it was like a dollar or two… We got the turkey, won the turkey…

Mary: I remember getting the goose, but I don't remember ever getting a turkey…

Mel: That would have been better anyhow …

Mary: But I do remember right before one of those Christmas programs, I think Marie Frederick brought her sled and everybody said, "Oh, come on, go down," and we went down past the school, past that big tree down there and down into Tiptons' pasture. Well, I wasn't used to that sled and I didn't make the turn and I hit that tree, and I was sore for the Christmas program that time. Surprised I didn't get killed …

Del: Ok, anything else? Are we winding down here? Nine o'clock …

John: Um-humm.

Del: You think so? John thinks so … One last word?

John: One last word.

Del: Ok, there it is. Anything anybody wants to say?

Maynard: He probably remembers the time we put leaves in Ma's privy. She wasn't too happy about that. She finally caught up with us. Remember that?

John: We got paddled that time, didn't we?

Maynard: Yeah, we got paddled when she caught us.

Mary: Remember the time they dug the new one? I think it was the last one we had. I was just a little kid, and I was down in there helping them, watching them dig, and I peed my pants, so they figured I was the first one to use it. (Laughter)

Mel: I went with Nowaks' daughter for a while and I came home one Halloween night and everybody was in bed and I thought, "Oh, man, that old man, he's afraid to get up on anything," so I took his milk cart and put it up clear on top of that great big barn down there, you know. I must have spent a half hour getting it up there. I'm in bed upstairs, you know, the next morning and somebody rattled on the door and Mom was cooking breakfast and she said, "Yeah, he's in bed"—I heard her say, "Yeah, he's in bed"—so she hollered at me, "Come down here," so I come down, and Nowak says, "Some idiot put my milk cart on the barn; I want you to take it down for me." (Laughter) So I went down. And I said, "Lawrence, you got a rope?" And he says, "No." I says, "Well, get away from that manure pile, here it comes," and I just let it loose and it went down in the manure pile. (Laughter) And another time, I think Ralph Frederick was along on that little deal … We took his cultivator, his walking plow or riding plow or whatever it was, and set it over the barbed wire fence, you know, and those shovels go through that barbed wire, and you've gotta take it apart to get 'em out. He was a little upset about that.

Del: It sounds like Halloween tricks …

Mel: Yeah, Halloween tricks …

Del: Upsetting privies …

Mary: Yeah, remember getting to school after Halloween night?

Del: Yeah, no privy … (Laughter)

John: They were upset over at school there … Were you still in school when Lester went up and said to John Judas, "How come you did that?"

Del: I don't remember that.

John: Lester asked John why he did that, and I guess he wasn't very happy about it.

Del: And taking the flagpole out of the … whatever it's called?

Maynard: Didn't he stick him in a posthole he was digging…?

John: I think so …

Maynard: … head first? (Laughter) Head first.

Mel: They never had a flag down there when I went to school.

Del: Really?

John: Yeah, I used to climb the flagpole all the time. The teacher got after me and then when the flag got caught: "Would you climb the flagpole?" (Laughter) I climbed the flagpole up at Berreman here about five, six years ago and I found out—I made it but I found out that was not a good thing to do. I was all winded by the time I got up there and got back down.

Maynard: It wasn't easy climbing those things either.

John: No, it wasn't.

Maynard: Do it all by hand, no place to put your feet.

Carolyn: Well, I wanted to say that I was the first one that went to high school and Dad didn't want me to go and live in town, and there was no bus and there was no way to get in to school, and that summer we were painting the house and I painted the shutters, dark green. I remember down by the clothesline and I was trying to figure out how I was gonna' get to town and back to go to school. Old Mrs. Elliott was gonna' teach that year—that was her first year—and she didn't drive, so … what was his name?

Del: Austen, yeah.

Carolyn: Austen Elliott. He worked at the hardware store, and he was gonna' drive her out and he was gonna' come out and get her at night, so I said, "Ah-ha, there's my ride: when he comes out, I'll go in with him and when he comes out to get her, I'll come home." And it worked out, but he never took me one inch out of the way, and when it rained or the road was bad, I walked the mile over to the hard road to meet him. He never took me to school; he came in, parked the car by the bank and I walked to school. But I got to school … I think the next year you drove …

John: Well, I took her in and brought you home.

Carolyn: Yeah, yeah. The next year you guys did it and then when you were in the field, sometimes it was dark before I got home, because you didn't come to get me after school.

John: I played a few too many games of pool …

Carolyn: Yeah, you used to go down and park and go in there with Ray Moshure and play pool, and I had to sit in the car. (Laughter) And when Maynard took me, I was always late. (Laughter) He had to go to the hardware store every time, and I'd sit in the car and I'd say, "Well now, let's see, is he gonna' be in there? Can I walk up to school, or should I wait for him?" I was always late, every time.

Mary: Remember when you [Del] tried to teach me how to drive so I could drive because …

Del: Brrrrr! (Laughter) Yeah.

Mary: ... I was old enough to get a license, but you weren't. You were just gonna' get a permit and then you were gonna' drive ...

Del: Yeah, that was the plan.

Mary: And every time I let the clutch out, I killed it ... (Laughter)

Del: Yeah. You finally did learn though.

Mary: Yeah, I learned, not on that car.

Del: Yeah. I think the clutch went out on that car. (Laughter)

Mary: I learned to drive in Chicago...

Mel: When I worked at Ford, you know, Harry Abrams had a 49 Ford with a stick in it and a trailer. He'd load that trailer with chickens, pile the back of the car full of eggs, and he'd burn up a clutch about every two months. I'd have to put a new clutch in that thing. So we traded in a car and there was a little kids' baseball bat about that long in there, and we gave that to his kid and I said, "Your old man puts his foot on that pedal ..."—he'd ride the clutch, you know, that's what he was doing—I said, "Your old man puts his foot on that pedal down there, you whack him across the knee with this ..." (Laughter) Every time he'd stop for a stop light, that kid would be beatin' ... (Laughter) He came back and he jumped all over me. He says, "What did you tell my kid?" "I don't know, what did I tell him?" (Laughter) He said, "You told him to beat me with that baseball bat." (Laughter)

Maynard: Sometimes I'd come in at 3 o'clock and meet Dad coming, g'tting' up, and I'd be goin' to bed. Kinda' frowned on that ... (Laughter)

Del: 3 o'clock, huh?

Mary: So how'd you get in then?

Del: What about climbing in a window?

Maynard: He used to lock the doors, and Mel climbed in the window a few times. (Laughter) If he could do it, I can do it too. (Laughter)

Someone (?): Wasn't there a step that was creaky too?

Maynard: So I did …

Del: I heard something about a creaky step.

Maynard: Some of the steps did creak, didn't they?

Mary: They did.

John: If I got home, and I looked at the clock and if it was about time for it to strike, I'd hold my finger on it so it wouldn't make any noise … (Laughter)

Maynard: They never heard me come home. (Laughter)

John: I'd sneak in and they never heard me. Even when I came in with the motorcycle, I'd coast in [Laughter], and they usually never heard me.

Mel: You remember him telling about when the girls, his sisters, were all home? And the one who used to sneak in—and Grandpa and Grandma never heard 'em—so Dad says, "I'll fix that," so he went and took a dishpan and with a pound of nails and put 'em up on the top step and ran a rope down and when he went to bed, then he tied it on the doorknob, and when they yanked that door open [Laughter], here came that bucket of nails, that basket of nails, down, and it must have made a horrible noise—you know how that would sound in the middle of the night when everything was quiet. So after that when they came in, why they'd slam a couple doors and things like that. (Laughter)

Del: Those are good promptings. Any others? Any other stories you've heard?

Terry (?): How about those weird bicycle stories, Mom? (Other talk unintelligible)

Carolyn: Bicycle story isn't anything … (Laughter) Well, the boys got a bicycle—Maynard and John. I don't know where they got it. It was a girl's bicycle, and I wanted them to teach me to ride the bike—and they wouldn't. They didn't want me to ride it. So when they were out doing something, I just practiced until I could ride it, and then when they came home, I said, "Come on, let me ride the bike; let me ride the bike." So I got on and rode. Just rode away …

Mel: You remember where we learned to ride, don't you? Down on Highway 78 there. Bob Wagner, you know, he had a real nice bike because he had delivered papers in Mt. Carroll, and when he was out to Fredericks—he was their cousin—and he was out there, and he left the bike so they brought it over here, and we went down 78 on Sunday afternoon; we learned to ride that bike down there on the highway. Dad and Mom weren't too happy about that when they found out we were down there on the highway learning to ride that bike.

John: I never learned to ride a bike. I learned to ride that motorcycle with Maynard—that old Indian, I think.

Maynard: I remember that old red one that didn't have any spillbars on. You were riding it up here in the field, and it got you down …

John: Yeah.

Maynard: … and couldn't get up. I had to pick it up off of you.

John: That old 28, was it?

Maynard: Yeah. Old Red One, we called it.

John: Yeah.

Mel: It was that old JD, wasn't it?

Maynard: Yeah. Worked at that dumb thing all week, tried to get the battery charged up so we could ride it a couple hours on Sunday. (Laughter)

Mel: I had that down to Hanover one time, and I had my 39 down there and I don't know how we had it down there but Allan, Allan Beyer, says, "Let me ride that thing," so he rides up the street, and you know, it just had a brush paint job on it and these couple girls Delbert and I were talking to came down and said, "Oh, look at that pretty red motorcycle," and Delbert says, "I don't believe this. Here we've got a couple of bikes that are only a couple years old and they want to ride that thing." (Laughter)

Someone (?): How about the garden story?

Del: The garden story?

Someone (?): Picking the flowers...

Del: Nobody knows the garden story ...

Mary: Yes, when my dear brothers didn't want me to go in and pick their flowers back behind the granary, so they rigged up a bucket of water. Didn't you ever hear that?

Del: Oh, I guess I have heard that.

Mary: And then they sent Carolyn to get me to go in, so they could go in the shop and watch. (Laughter) Of course, when I opened the gate, the water spilled down on me.

Mel: I thought you were going in to eat strawberries.

Carolyn: No, they each had a flower patch, and they didn't want us to pick the flowers 'cause they wanted them to go to seed so they could have the seed ...

Mary: They just didn't want me in their flowerbed. (Laughter) That's the kind of brothers I had! (Laughter) Remember the time you were down behind the brooder house picking strawberries? Clyde Shriner was along.

Maynard: Yeah, he was behind the chicken house.

Carolyn: Yeah.

Mary: You kids got out so Mother could see, and she hollered down and said, "You better quit eating strawberries; you won't be able to eat any dinner."

Mel: I think she hollered, "You kids get out of the strawberry patch." Clyde thought that was just funnier than heck. She didn't see him. (Laughter)

Carolyn: But she did say, "spoil your dinner," and at dinnertime he says, "I wonder how they'd eat if they had really spoiled their dinner." (Laughter)

Mary: Let's hear the cider story ...

Del: The cider story! (Laughter)

Mary: That I don't remember either. (Laughter)

Carolyn: Well, we had a bunch of ...

Mary: Bad cider ...

Carolyn: ...a bunch of cider apple trees out here in the orchard, and every year Dad took a load of them and made cider, and he had, I guess he had fermented cider.

Mel: Yeah, this was cured stuff ...

Mary: Bad cider ...

Carolyn: And it was in a nice barrel and a nice spigot. And everybody was out ...

John: We were planting potatoes.

Carolyn: ... planting potatoes. I don't know, somebody asked if we were supposed to be taking care of Del, but I don't remember Del being there. I don't know where you were ...

John: Yeah, he was here.

Del: I was here? I didn't know …

Carolyn: Where were you? Where was he?

Mary: I don't remember …

Carolyn: Do you remember him?

Mel: No, I don't know.

John: He left the cellar door open and he went down there and …

Carolyn: Well, no, but I don't remember Del being here.

John: Yeah, he was here. He was about 4 years old …

Carolyn: Where was he? Well, he must have …

John: And Mother was so upset because he could have fallen down there.

Carolyn: Well, anyway, Mary and I went down to the cellar and it was so much fun to see the cider come out of the spigot. 'Course we drank enough of it to get drunk (Laughter) and in the other cellar …

Mary: Probably didn't take much.

Carolyn: No, I don't think it did take much. We didn't drink much. We weren't doing it to drink it; we were doing it to watch it come out, but you couldn't just dump it out. But the big problem was that Mother had the incubator set up in the other cellar and for whatever reason—I don't know—I took one of the lamps out and they were kerosene …

John: They were kerosene lamps…

Carolyn: Yeah, and it went out so I knew I had to light it again. So I came up to the kitchen and got matches and I guess I konked out in the middle of the floor. Mary was konked out in the cellar, but the cellar door was open.

Mary: She remembers it. I don't remember.

Carolyn: I remember it. And I asked Mel the other day and he says, "Yeah, Mother found, Mother came in and she got a little hysterical, and when Dad came in he knew right away what it was. We were put to bed. She said …

Mel: "No more cider!"

Carolyn: Yeah, but we never heard anything about it again. It was never mentioned.

Mel: Well, you know, he had a, I suppose it might have been a 10 gallon jug with a small neck on it, kind of a unique jug. They were cleaning the back basement out and it got shoved underneath the steps. Remember that? Anyhow, Dad looked for that and he thought it had got broken or maybe she got rid of it or something, never really quizzed anybody down but he couldn't find it, so it ran along a couple years and he's down there cleaning out one time and, "Oh, there's my jug," you know, and boy, this cider, you know, about three or four years old, boy, it was pretty wild! (Laughter) And Mom's cousin, George Randecker, was working, helping Dad pick corn, and so he gave George about a double shot in the bottom of a water glass, and he says, "Harry, haven't you got much of that?" and he says, "Oh, yeah, I've got a whole 10-gallon jug of it." "Well," he says, "You know, I could drink a couple glasses of that and I'd show you how to pick corn this afternoon." (Laughter) So Dad gave him what he wanted, and he drank it at noontime, and they go out to pick corn and I guess they were pickin' on the ridge back there—two rows back and three the other way, or something like that—and Dad could really pick corn, and he goes across there and he comes back, and George was only about halfway across the first time, and Dad's been back and met him there. And he said George'd start at the bottom of the stalk and he'd reach up [Laughter] and follow it up and find an ear and then he'd husk the ear of corn out and he'd throw it where he thought the wagon was [Laughter] and he said I stopped and said, "George, what are you doin'?" "Well, I'm pickin' corn. What's it look like?" (Laughter) He said he never did get that load of corn picked. And Mother was a little upset with him. She said, "You shouldn't have given him that." Dad said, "Well, he wanted it." (Laughter)

Del: And making root beer was a popular thing for a while there too, wasn't it?

Carolyn: That was John and Maynard.

Mel: I never got in on that.

Del: You didn't get in on that?

Mel: No.

Maynard: We made root beer, supposed to let it set a couple days till the yeast gets a chance to work; then you're supposed to put it where it was cold, so it wouldn't go any further. And I guess we didn't get it out of there in time, and it started blowin' up. (Laughter) Kinda' made a mess.

Del: Wanta' add anything to that?

John: That's about the way it was. (Laughter)

Del: Well, we've talked about our parents, we've talked about each other and growing up, talked about school … We haven't talked about neighbors. We could talk about [Laughter] things we remember about neighbors.

Somebody (Bernice ?): Now you're meddling.

Del: Now we're meddling. Anybody remember anything about neighbors you want to talk about? Any stories?

Mel: The only thing I remember is putting the cart on top of the barn.

Del: Yeah, ok. Neighbors? Fredericks? Kantlehners? Nowaks? Potters? Who else? Schmidts? Maders?

John: Hardly any of the old neighbors left any more. Ernie Katzenberger is about the only one. She passed away here a year or so ago. He's still living, not in very good shape.

Del: Well, that one didn't go far, did it? The neighbors. I guess we've about run our course here. Do you have something, Maynard?

Maynard: I remember Tiptons going over to Randeckers and he'd get 'em drunked up and I remember Mother saying she didn't think that was too smart, if something had happened to 'em …

Carolyn: We used to go over quite a bit, didn't we, over to Dan Randeckers? …

Mel: Yeah. His brothers used to go to town, and they'd come home and they'd have a pint and say, "Well, we better have a little drink; we just had a birthday." And Dad would say, "Whose birthday is it?" and they'd point at each other, you know (Laughter). Every time they'd go to town they'd have a birthday. (Laughter)

Del: Well, we've heard the story about a couple of girls who instead of coming directly home would go in the opposite direction … Somebody would tell, I guess. Anybody want to talk about that? Somebody would tell Mother where they had gone?

Mel: Who was that?

Carolyn: That was me and Mary. School'd be out and we'd walk with Mabel and LaVonne. We'd go the other way, and Maynard would run home as fast as he could come and say, "The girls are going the other way again." (Laughter) Of course, we were always late, so she scolded us for that. One time, I think, in the wintertime, we went up there along the crick and broke through the ice and got all wet and came home with our feet half frozen.

Mary: I don't remember that. The only time I remember was going along with LaVonne over to Schuberts and her mother was baking those cookies with, those raisin-filled cookies, and we thought they were so good we got the recipe. (See the recipe in Chapter VII.)

Carolyn: I think we stayed over night. I don't think …

Mary: I don't think we did.

Carolyn: Yeah, I remember we did stay over night …

Mary: No, I think we came home and Mother sorta growled because we were so late.

Carolyn: We never went that far.

Mary: Yeah, we did. (Laughter) Yeah, we did.

Del: Disagreement here tonight … (Laughter)

Carolyn: We went over, we stayed over there …

Mary: No.

Carolyn: … but we never …

Mary: I don't ever remember staying at Schuberts overnight.

Carolyn: I do. I remember when Roy Schubert had his back hurt. Yup, we did.

Mary: I just remember going over there and coming back so late. Mother was all upset because it took us so long to get home.

Carolyn: We never went all the way over to Schuberts because they lived a long way over there.

Del: Barb has a question.

Barbara: I want to know what you did when you celebrated birthdays or Christmas …

Del: That's a good question. Who wants to share? I don't ever remember celebrating birthdays. We never had birthday parties …

Carolyn: Oh, we did too. We always had cake and ice cream.

John: We had cake and ice cream …

Barb: What'd she make?

John: Nut cake …

Del: Not a party though … .

Carolyn: No, we never had a party.

Mary: I never had ice cream except the one time I think somebody buried ice over here in the pigeon pen, so it kept and we made ice cream.

Carolyn: Yeah, John and I had the ice cream because our birthdays are in December …

Mary: Yeah, mine is in April so …

Somebody (Terry?): Who was it who thought the ice cream was going to be dirty because …

Carolyn: Well, that was our cousin from Rockford. She was looking out of the window and she saw me getting the ice out of the tank, and she said, "I'm not gonna' eat any of that ice cream because she's getting the ice out of the horse tank." (Laughter) We didn't even have horses. (Laughter)

Mel: Thank God for small favors. (Laughter) Dumbest animal in the world.

Mary: Yeah, the one that almost killed me?

Mel: Yeah.

Carolyn: Well, you were where you weren't supposed to be. You were hanging on the fence.

Mel: That same team ran away from me and Maynard and tore up Dad's best mower. It didn't take too much after that to convince him to buy a good tractor, did it?

Mary: Was that Barney and Nigger?

Del: Barney and who? Say what? (Laughter)

Mary: Barney and Nigger. Was that Barney and Nigger?

Mel: No, it was that big roan, wasn't it?

Mary: The only horses I remember are Barney and Nigger.

Mel: I know after Dad came out, it was lunchtime, and Dad came out and he saw them running between the straw pile and the fence and there was only room to go through when the cyclebar was up, and the cyclebar was down. And, you know, it wiped that mower out, and he unhitched them. They ran all the way down to the timber, and they ran straddle of a little hickory tree down there and they just stood there. And so he unhitched them and he brought 'em back and the corn was about that tall out here in this 10-acre field. While we ate lunch he harrowed that 10 acres. He'd look at his footprints and they were as far apart as from here to the end of that table (Laughter), you know, and Mom says, "He's gonna' kill those horses," and I said, "Well, it won't be a big loss if he does, you know." But every time they'd slow up, he'd take the lines and whack them one over the tail: "Run now, if you want to run!" (Laughter)

Maynard: I know we spent the afternoon fixing the fence where they wiped it out. They ran right along the fence and busted off the posts.

Mel: Yeah, it tore the fence up and tore the mower up too. It ripped that cyclebar right off of it.

John: Yeah, I found pieces of it in the field there quite a few years after that. Somebody has been bugging me about telling a story about Maynard … On Saturday night … Everybody went to town on Saturday night. And I saw Bernice standing on the street corner and I thought "a good chance," and asked, "You want a ride, Bernice?" So we were driving around town and Maynard spotted us and it kinda' shook him up, I think, and next morning he says, "You leave her alone; she's my girl," and he had never gone out with her. (Laughter) So I don't know if it was my fault that I forced him into (Laughter) going with her. Coulda' been, but it turned out good.

Del: Any word on that?

Maynard: Probably true. (Laughter)

Mel: Then Mel, he comes home and he says Maynard was the only one who could get back in that area.

Barbara: How many cars did you wear out going there?

John: Well, he wore out one, I'll tell you.

Bernice: It was worn out when he got it. (Laughter)

Maynard: She always said it was worn out when I got it. (Laughter)

John: It came from Charlie Wolf, didn't it?

Maynard: Yeah, that coupe did. (Laughter)

Del: Well, the other part of the question was Christmas. We haven't talked about that, what we did for Christmas.

John: Nothing really special.

Del: Well, we always had presents ...

Mary: We always had a tree.

John: Usually, well ...

Del: You guys went out and got a tree several times.

Mary: I remember a couple trees ...

John: We always had a tree though.

Mary: We got one present. And I remember the time Carolyn and I snooped and found ours. It was a cheap dresser set. I got a pink one; she got a blue one. A mirror and brush and comb. And that was the worst Christmas we ever had, because we knew what we were gettin'. (Laughter)

Mel: Shouldn't have snooped.

John: Mother made stuff for us, which, you know, was good. I know they didn't have the money to buy a lot of stuff.

Del: Well, we got clothes that she ordered from Sears, Roebuck or Montgomery Ward, right?

Carolyn: That wasn't really our Christmas presents though.

Mary: No, I don't remember that either.

Carolyn: I don't remember getting clothes for Christmas …

Mary: A doll or a coloring book or something like that, nothin' much. When I think about what kids get now, but we didn't think we were being cheated.

Del: Anything you want to say, Mel? No? Ok. Any other questions?

Somebody (Barb?): What were your favorite foods?

Mary: Your favorite what?

Del: Foods, foods.

Somebody (Barb?): What things did you like? I know she did a lot of cooking and canning. I remember that.

John: I loved her fried chicken, chickens she raised, and they were so good with potatoes and gravy. It was really, really good.

(Unintelligible comment)

John: What do *you* think? We even ate … I even liked the feet. Did you ever hear of eatin' the feet?

Del: Oh, they were good …

John: Yeah, yeah, they were.

Del: And I think Maynard's favorite food was cottage cheese, wasn't it? (Laughter)

Mary: Butter.

Several: Butter. (Laughter)

Del: What was your favorite?

Maynard: Well, I liked that chicken, carrot soup.

Del: Carrot soup, oh.

Maynard: Mouldresher.

Del: MOULDRESHER, ooh.

Mel: Yeah, oh yeah, that was good.

Maynard: Noodles, homemade noodles.

Del: Stuffed noodles.

Somebody: What was it called?

Del: Mouldresher. Not "bowel," "moul." (Laughter)

Mary: Chicken noodle soup was good.

Carolyn: Bernice makes a good mouldresher…

Del: Revel soup. Remember revel soup?

Mel: Oh yeah. You can get that at the restaurant once in a while.

John: Edna makes a good revel soup.

Carolyn: You know where to come now, don't you?

Maynard: She makes that too.

John: Since I've been sick she's made it quite a few times for me.

Mary: The chicken noodle soup was good, because you can't make it with the chickens you buy. You can't make the kind of noodle soup we used to have.

Mel: Well, you've got to get stewing hens.

Carolyn: I think the kuchen and the plum stuff she used to make, she used to make that at Easter time.

Del: Yeah, the "pluma stuff"—that was your favorite (John's), wasn't it?

John: I'd come home on Saturday night and eat a piece of two of that before I went to bed.

Del: Remember the pies she used to make and then cut them in fourths? She'd make two of them, and then there was one extra piece left over—and it was always a controversy over who gets the extra piece.

Carolyn: But where did she get those plums that time?

John: They were wild plums …

Carolyn: Yeah, I know but they were down there …

John: Down here at the corner there were some plums and there were some over on what's Maynard's along the road there.

Mel: Up on top of that hill there, yeah.

John: Back on Boneses there were a bunch of them …

Maynard: Back at Boneses, the Chickasaws, they were a little bigger than the other ones …

Carolyn: Well, they were sour plums, and it made it perfect.

Del: I guess the pie controversy arose after Mel left. It was working out …

Mary: Yeah, because …

Del: There were only seven of us then so there'd be one piece left over …

Mel, you haven't told us what your favorite food was.

Mel: Sauerkraut and dumplings.

Del: Same as Dad's… That used to be his favorite.

Carolyn: Pork cooked in the sauerkraut …

Mel: Yeah, spareribs, spareribs, sauerkraut, dumplings …

John: She used to cook the pig legs too.

Mel: Pighocks, yeah

Carolyn: Oh, I didn't like that.

Mel: Oh, they were good.

Carolyn: Well, not the skin and the …

Mel: Oh yes. (Laughter) What's the matter with you?

Del: Remember the liverworst? That was good.

Mel: Yeah.

John: Yeah, but I was aggravated at him that he always kept those pigs that had only one nut (Laughter) and the other one was up in the belly, and then he butchered those. And I mean they stunk like an old boar. (Laughter) Let somebody else eat them.

Mel: Mom called them "the old originals." (Laughter)

John: Why he thought we should eat those … Let somebody else eat 'em.

Mel: I've run into that in restaurants already where it smells like that.

John: I remember when I was working for Paul Law, I came home for dinner and the minute I walked in the house, she said, "I have pork chops here but I think they're spoiled," and I said, "There're not spoiled; they're just out of an old boar." (Laughter) Get 'em past your nose. (Laughter)

Mary: Favorite food? I said chicken and noodles. We'd go out and kill the chicken, and Mother'd make the noodles. And nobody could cut noodles like Mother.

Carolyn: I chopped many a head off of a rooster.

Mary: And so did I.

Del: So yours was chicken and …

Carolyn: No, I said kucha. (*Kuchen?*) She always made that at Easter.

Somebody (?): What was that?

Several: Coffee cake.

Somebody (?): Is that the German word for it?

Did you all speak German?

Carolyn: No.

Del: Just a few words here and there.

Mel: I used to talk it real good when I first started to school. In fact, the teacher said to my Mom one time, "I wish I knew what he says when he gets a little upset." (Laughter) Mom said, "It's probably just as well that you don't." (Laughter)

Carolyn: Wasn't it Maynard that the teacher'd ask a question and he'd answer her in German? (Laughter)

Mel: The first year she couldn't get him to talk! (Laughter) Right?

Del: Well, anything else anybody wants to hear about?

Mike (?): I'd like to know how John was the only one who could sneak in here without anybody knowin' about it and none of the other brothers and sisters figured that out.

Somebody (?): And how about Del? We haven't heard about his dating life.

Del: My dating life? Most of that was after I left here …

Mary: And we didn't sneak out, so … Where would we go? We didn't have a car.

Mike (?): Neighborhood? (Laughter)

Mary: You mean like Marvin Judas or somebody? (Laughter)

Mel: Windy Ward.

Del: Windy Ward, oh yeah.

John: Oh yeah, Windy Ward.

Carolyn: Well, rumor has it that you brought a girl here.

Del: I brought a GIRL here?

Somebody (?): … from Savanna…

Del: Yes, I dated a girl from Savanna for a while, yes.

John: You had trouble getting away from her too, didn't you?

Del: Well (Laughter), her mother sort of thought it would be good for us to get hitched, and so when we broke up her mother wasn't very happy about it, so she wrote some rather nasty letters, said some rather nasty things—but that's not a very good story. (Laughter) We'd rather hear some of the other dating stories. Dating? Matrimony?

(Unintelligible talk)

Mary: We would stay home and work all summer and wouldn't see anybody until it was time for school to start and then you had to get reacquainted with the school kids.

Carolyn: We didn't do anything.

Del: We thought going to town was a big event, just going to town once a week or even if that …

Mary: The first time I ever went to a movie was when Mel came home from the Navy and took us. We went to see "God is My Co-Pilot." Remember that?

Del: Dennis Day

Carolyn: I remember that.

Del: I remember it too.

Mary: But we were pretty proud of our big brother 'cause he was in the Navy.

Carolyn: Yeah, we had that little flag out there in that bedroom window with one star on it.

Mel: They've got that again now, you know.

Carolyn: Yeah, we were pretty proud of that.

Del: Yeah, we didn't know any better. (Laughter)

Mary: I don't know what he thought about it, but when Mother'd write letters we'd write letters, "How are you? We are fine" or something like that we'd start off. We had to write to our big brother.

Maynard: Mother'd write a letter every Sunday.

Mary: Yup. She did that to everybody that left.

Del: Yeah, she did. Every Sunday afternoon she'd write letters to us.

Carolyn: Yeah, she did.

Del: Faithfully.

(Unintelligible talk)

Del: Sibling rivalry. Ooooh. Which two fought the most?

Carolyn: We didn't fight at all, did we?

Mary: I don't think we …

V. Kehl Talk

"I wish to remark,
That my language is plain."
  (Bret Harte, "Plain Language from Truthful James")

"When you're lying awake with a dismal headache,
and repose is taboo'd by anxiety,
I conceive you may use any language you choose
to indulge in, without impropriety."
       (W. S. Gilbert, *Iolanthe*)

"Individuality of expression is the beginning and end of
all art."   (Goethe, *Proverbs in Prose*)

"Slang is language that takes off its coat, rolls up its
sleeves, spits on its hands, and gets to work."
       (Carl Sandburg)

The Apostle Paul admonishes believers to let our "speech always be with grace seasoned with salt" (Colossians 4:6). Kehl talk through the years has not always been especially graceful, but it has almost always been salty, that is, sharp, witty, sometimes racy and earthy, sometimes scatological (dealing with feces, excrement, bodily functions, and other grossology) but definitely not profane or obscene. No profanity or obscenity was permitted or practiced in our family. (I can remember hearing only one, single unquestionably "obscene" expression during all those years growing up in this family, an expression uttered by an older brother, back in the field, well out of parental earshot, and I was obviously duly shocked, as suggested by the fact that I still remember it, but, at the same time, I wonder how many members of other families could name so few. And I can remember uttering a bit of profanity I had heard at school; my mother gave me a look of reproach that burned into my psyche—and I never repeated it.) This chapter is an attempt to compile and analyze words and expressions which have been used exclusively, or as much as it's possible to determine such exclusivity, by and in the Kehl family. We might say, with slight variation on Lord Sands in Shakespeare's *King Henry the Eighth*, "If I chance to talk a little wild, forgive me; I had it from my family." Much of Kehl talk is "wild" but not necessarily in a negative sense.

Many of the examples are colloquialisms or slang, illustrating Carl Sandburg's statement that slang is "language that takes off its coat, rolls up its sleeves, spits on its hands, and gets to work." It should be no surprise that Kehl talk was especially earthy, formed as it has been from the earth of the midwestern farmland. It's the down-to-earth, simple, natural, straightforward language of realism shaped by the hardscrabble life on the farm. Unrelenting toil in the sweltering heat and sultriness of summer (the kind described by Hamlin Garland in such stories from *Main-Travelled Roads* as "Among the Corn Rows") and the bitter cold of winter does not promote elegant, refined, polished talk. The line between crude and crass may be subjective and thin. Kehl talk may at times have been vulgar and maybe gross but not indecent, indelicate but not ribald, unadorned and unrefined but not coarse, natural but not obscene, earthy but not profane, though some examples may be admittedly debatable.

Minced Forms

"'Earthy but not profane,' huh?" "What do you mean by that?" someone may ask. As noted above, obscenity and profanity were not permitted in our family. Profanity (from the Latin *pro* + *fanum* literally "before the temple"—therefore, the kind of language not to be used near the temple or place of worship) is language showing disrespect or contempt for sacred things, irreverent, desecrating, debasing, even blasphemous. This is not to claim, though, that our family never used what linguists call "minced forms," that is, "distortions in language that result when the human impulse to swear is held in check by religious or social prohibitions. The usual compromise is a word or phrase that suggests rather than states, that at once approaches the forbidden but shies away from it." (I've quoted here from a text, written by the professor I had in a graduate course on the history of the English language at the University of Wisconsin, Madison.) Such minced forms include: *gosh, golly, gee, gee whiz, gee whillikers, gad, goodness gracious, for goodness sake, darn, dad-burned, dad-blasted, dad-blamed, doggone it, gol-darn, gol-durned, jeez, jeepers creepers, jiminy crickets, jeeminy crickets, criminy, criminutly, cripes, for crying out loud, for pete's sake, judas priest, go jump in the lake*, plus others and versions of these. I recall using and hearing some of these minced forms, but most often our interjections were limited to *shoot, shucks, gee whiz*, or *nuts*. Many are euphemisms, that is, words or phrases in which indirectness replaces direct offensiveness.

Scatological Expressions

Another category of expressions is the scatological, those dealing with bodily functions, private parts, and excrement—admittedly rather gross but certainly not profane. Often they referred to parts of the anatomy, particularly American slang like "butt" (shortened form of "buttocks") (or what the British call "the bum"), "rear" (or "rear-end"), "rump," "tail," "behind" (or "bottom"), "posterior," "seat," "fanny," and (rare) "keester." Specific expressions include: "Don't be such a sore a--"; "You've got it all bass-ackward"; "Peddling hard to give his a-- a ride" (Maynard's description of bicycle riding); "Kiss my foot three joints high"; "He doesn't know his a-- from a hole in the ground."

The old Anglo-Saxon word for excrement, s---, surely sounds more offensive than the French *merde*, but as Shakespeare's Juliet says to Romeo, "What's in a name? That which we call a rose / By any other name would smell as sweet"—or, in this case, s--- by any other name would smell as foul. Expressions in this category include: "He thinks his s--- don't stink"; "Not worth a s---"; "It scared him s---less"; "Don't s--- your pants"; "Grinnin' like a monkey eatin' s---"; "Eat and sleep and s--- behind the fence"; "He's got the scoots!"; "He runs off at the mouth, got diarrhea of the mouth"; "Go to the s---house" (or privy or *heisley*); "Don't cut your foot on that cow-patty." The boys never said in a prissy way, "I am going to the bathroom" (which we didn't have anyway) but, "Gonna go take a s---."

Flatulence is probably common in most families, especially those with boys. It gave rise (no pun intended) to such expressions as these: "No need to tear it; I'll take the whole remnant"; "Who f---ed? Smells like gun blue!"; and such similes as "Jumpin' around like a f--- in a frying pan" and "He moves like a f--- in a whirlwind." Another bodily function produced such expressions as "Gotta' go take a leak" and "Better to be p---ed off than p----ed on!" Crude but not necessarily crass are such expressions as "Slick as snot on a door knob"; "Stop grubbin'; use your snot-rag"; and "Which is worse: blowin' it on the ground or blowin' it in a rag and carryin' it around in your pocket?"

Animal Comparisons

It shouldn't be at all surprising that on a farm so many expressions are comparisons with animals. One unique expression was, "They'll be here till the **cows** come home to roost." Someone may say, "Oh, but cows don't roost! Only chickens, other fowl, and birds roost." Oh, thanks for clearing that up! Isn't that just the point? Another fairly common expression was, "That's the tune the ole cow died on," often used to describe Kate Smith's singing or opera arias. Expressions using comparisons with **pigs** include, "Don't be such a pig" (used when excessive portions of food were taken), "Stop hoggin' all the candy" (or pie or cake or whipped cream), and "Eatin' high on the hog." "Worthless as tits on a boar" was an effective simile, for obvious reasons. Election time evoked the expression "He'd vote for a spotted hog if the Democrats [or Republicans, for that matter] put one up." **Horses**, even though in later years they were generally detested by the boys and gave way to tractors, also evoked some comparisons, such as "Stop horsein' around" and "Hold your horses," as well as these euphemistic expressions, "Gotta' go see a man about a horse" and "Better close the barn door [i.e., zipper fly]—horse'll get out." With **dogs** always being fairly numerous and ubiquitous on the farm, one would think this species might prompt more expressions, these being the only ones I can remember: "He's as crooked as a dog's hind leg," another vivid simile, and "He left with his tail between his legs." Two similes prompted by **chickens** are: "Mad as an ole settin' hen" (and if that one doesn't resonate, you probably haven't tried to reach under a setting hen to check for eggs) and "Scarce as hens' teeth." "That really gets my **goat**," meaning that something causes annoyance, frustration, or downright anger was a common expression but probably not limited to our family, though I don't ever remember hearing it used by anyone outside the family.

Put-Downs and Come-Uppance

Often the motivation for certain expressions has been put-downs (belittling remarks or crushing retorts) and come-uppance (a deserved verbal punishment or linguistic retribution), such as: "Ain't you gettin' a little too big for your britches?"; "He couldn't hit the broad side of a barn!"; "You move around like an old man 90 years old!"; "I'll knock you into the middle of next week!"; "He doesn't amount to a hill of beans"; "Crazy as all get out"; "We all put our pants on one leg at a time"; "He's got the nose trouble" (meaning he's too curious, too inquisitive about other people's business); "He's just talkin' through his hat" (what he says is not reliable).

Seasons, Passage of Time

Again, it shouldn't be surprising that life on a farm often focused on the seasons and the passage of time (and the *Concise Oxford English Dictionary* recently noted that the most commonly used word in the English language is *time*). Kehl farm talk produced such expressions as these: "Corn should be knee-high by the 4th of July"; "When wind blows over the oat stubbles, it's movin' toward fall"; "By the end of the season, everybody's fed out on strawberries" (or raspberries or blackberries or grapes or apples); and "The sun still sets in Rob's timber" (Dad's expression about the constancy of nature and passage of time).

Death as an inevitable season of life produced these expressions: "One of these days he's gonna' stay layin'"; "He's gonna' be a goner"; "Deader'n a doornail"; "Just kicked the bucket" (or "Croaked"). Along with the seasons, weather itself produced the following: "It's colder'n all git out"; "It's makin' ugly" (Dad's expression); "Looks like a real gully-washer"; and "It's cold enough to freeze the n--- off a brass monkey."

Food

Food and eating were often metaphors in such expressions as "That's just the berries"; "Food enough to feed threshers"; "Sauerkraut is good for what ails yuh"; "Dumplings light as a feather"; "He doesn't amount to a hill of beans."

Figurative Language

One of the reasons Kehl talk is so vivid is its frequent use of various kinds of figurative language, such as the **simile**, a comparison using "like" or "as." Here are some examples: "He's fat as a tick"; "Scarce as hens' teeth"; "Goin' down the road like a house afire"; "Crooked as a dog's hind leg"; "Mad as an ole settin' hen"; "Dumplings light as a feather"; "Slower than molasses in January" (may not be exclusive to our family). **Metaphors**, comparisons or analogies identifying one thing with another, are also well represented, such as: "He's got a lead foot" (heavy on the accelerator); "Get the lead out" (Don't be so slow); "He's driving the puddle-jumper." Another example of figurative language is the **synecdoche**, a figure of speech in which a part signifies the whole or the whole a part, as in these examples: "He doesn't have two coins to rub together"; "I ain't seen hide nor hair of him"; "The sun still sets in Rob's timber." Closely related to the synecdoche is **metonymy**, a figure of speech in which something closely associated stands for a thing—for example: "She's had a tough row to hoe"; "You made your bed; now lay in it"; "Keep your shirt (or pants) on"; "That's just the berries."

Aphorism

An aphorism is a concise statement of a principle or precept in vivid words. What Texas author Larry McMurtry has said of cowboys may also be true of Illinois farmers: "Cowboys are aphorists. Whenever possible they turn their observations into aphorisms. Some are brilliant aphorists … ; one is proud to steal from them. I plucked a nice one several years ago: 'A woman's love is like the morning dew: it's just as apt to fall on a horse turd as it is on a rose.'" Here are some examples from the Kehl family: "Turn out the lights before you burn a hole in the day" (Dad's); "What you don't have in your hand, you can't throw away"; "If you don't expect too much, you won't be disappointed" (Mother's).

Coined words

Probably every family has its own hoard of specially coined words, those manufactured by almost every member of the family, some catching on and repeated, others used for certain occasions and then dropped, maybe to replaced by still others. We seemed to have an extra measure of our share, such as "He got all **boogered up**" (that is, banged up, battered, bruised); "What'd you **driller** all over your shirt?" (spill, drip); "It's only eight o'clock and you're already *gapping*. Why don't you go to bed?" (yawning); "Stop **grubbin'**" (picking your nose); "An old **junker**" (a vehicle that's a piece of junk, worthless); "It's **makin' ugly**" (the weather is getting inclement; a storm is brewing). One seems to be an example of onomatopoeia, that is, formation of a word by imitating the natural sound associated with it, echoic—"Stop your **yummering**" (a discontented, complaining sound made by a combination of whining, moaning, groaning, whimpering, crabbing, fussing, grumbling, and bawling). I remember "yummering" as a little kid when I was hungry, tired, sleepy, frustrated, and bored.

Every member of the family originated and used certain signature expressions, leaving his or her trademark on each. Dad had quite an array of expressions, probably more than anyone else in the family. A common expression of his, perhaps reflecting his philosophy of life, was "It's only through life." Others were: "Night'll bring 'em home"; "They always gotta' stay till the last dog is hung and the rope is put away"; "I could lift (or eat) that if it was only half that size"; "You move around like an old man 90 years old"; "Turn out the lights before you burn a hole in the day"; "The sun still sets in Rob's timber"; "He as crazy as all get out"; "That hurts like fury"; "That really plays hob"; "What kinda' riggin' fits there?" "He put it on cattywampus"; "It's makin' ugly"; "He can kiss my foot three joints high"; "No need to tear it; I'll take the whole remnant."

A common interjection was "Ahhh Yeahhh" (I remember both Dad and John saying it), apparently expressing something between mild frustration and resignation.

Mother had such expressions as these: "Oooooo, it's hot!"; "Gonna' scratch in a little lettuce"; "That old rip (or *schlepper*)"; "You great big goose!"; "One of these days he just gonna' stay layin'"; "If you don't expect too much, you won't be disappointed"; "What you don't have in your hand, you can't throw away." Others include these from Maynard: "He's got the nose trouble" and "Peddlin' hard to give his a-- a ride"; these from John: "Mamma, make him leave me alone!"; "I trust him about as far as I could throw him by his leg"; "Gonna' dig a hole and pull the hole in after me"; "Darn thing never was any good"; "How's comes?" (John); and Mary's response when, sick, she was asked if she wanted something to eat): "I *could* eat a banana."

German expressions (or variations)

Another category of expressions is German terms or their variations. When Mel and Maynard started to school, they spoke as much German as English. Through the years, as we were growing up, we often heard German expressions, but, of course, they faded and became less frequent with the passing years. Here are some common examples:

schlepper (slop)
luminzimmer (linen closet)
dohepitz (something)
grutzeli(scrub)
dumkopf (dumbhead)
dumheida (foolishness)
sheiskopf (s---head)
orshluck (a--hole)
macha bisly (hurry up)
hund (dog)
nichts wieder nichts (nothing, again nothing)
donner regnen (thunder rain)
dunderockem (thunderstorm)
strumpfly (stocking)
idalop stinks (bragging stinks)

stehl [something on] (get into trouble, get into mischief)
wundenaus (a silly, impractical invention or object)
seitspretripe (pastime)
nix noots (mischievous)
doppic (??)

Food:
mauldresher (stuffed noodles)
apfel cholat (apple pudding)
spotzel (egg noodle)
kucha (coffee cake)
fett dotsure (fat patty)

The double advice of figures as diversified as Lewis Carroll and Lord Chesterfield might well serve as a fitting conclusion here. Carroll writes in *Alice's Adventures in Wonderland*, "Take care of the sense, and the sounds will take care of themselves," whereas Lord Chesterfield wrote in a letter to his son, "Mind not what people say, but how they say it." If these two pieces of advice seem contradictory, maybe that's in part what makes Kehl talk "a little wild." But at least we talked.

VI: Telling Tales Out of School

"No more pencils, no more books,
No more teachers' dirty looks!"
                    (Popular doggerel, often chanted at the end of the school year)

"School days, school days,
Good old golden rule days,
Reading and writing and 'rithmetic—
Taught to the tune of the hickory stick."
                    (Popular ditty, often sung at the end of the school year)

"And then the whining school-boy, with his satchel
And shining morning face, creeping like a snail
Unwillingly to school."
                    (Shakespeare, *As You Like It*)

"I have had playmates, I have had companions,
In my days of childhood, in my joyful school days—
All, all are gone, the old familiar faces."
                    (Charles Lamb, *Old Familiar Faces*)

"I have never let my schooling interfere with my education."
                    (Mark Twain)

"A schoolboy's tale," Lord Byron wrote in *Childe Harold's Pilgrimage*, is but "the wonder of an hour" and then is gone and passed away, "dim with the mist of years." So it may be with the tales recounted here, whether by or about the schoolboy and his school. But whatever the "wonder" and the transience of the tales, these were formative years of our lives spent in grades 1-8 in a one-room country school.

The school had an illustrious, maybe even pretentious, name which probably few ever gave any thought to—"Sage." How "sage" *was* it or any of its pupils—"profoundly wise, discerning, prudent, judicious, showing good judgment"? Or was it named after Russell Sage, the American financier? Or after some now-unknown family named Sage? Or after the plant or shrub belonging to the mint family? Or after the sage grouse hen or sage sparrow or sage thrasher? Not likely any of these. Maybe just a misnomer. (A recent study by the Manhattan Institute, a so-called educational "think-tank," reports a sharp drop in schools being named after presidents—less than five percent nationally—and more being named after nature or natural features. Maybe Sage was ahead of its time, after all, if it got its name from a plant or bird.)

Dad attended Sage School through 3ʳᵈ grade, then stayed home to help in the field during the spring and fall, whereas his sisters attended regularly. He served on the local Sage District school board and helped hire teachers for Sage School. The districts were formulated by a distance of three to four miles from the school—walking distance. The schoolhouse itself is located about a half mile west of the Kehl farm, down one hill, up another, and down again, situated at the bottom of a small grassy slope, its door with protective roof overhang, three full windows and a half window facing east. The door opens into a small cloakroom used for hanging coats, storing overshoes, and stashing lunchboxes on a small table. Opposite the entrance is another door into the woodshed, used for storing kindling and coal for the furnace, and an attic. In the schoolroom itself, the furnace is to the right in the back, with four rows of pupil seats mounted on wooden slats, five or six seats in each row, and with the teacher's desk and swivel-chair in front, the "recitation bench" to the side. (Maynard says that when he first attended school, the seats were not mounted; this was done when he was in the middle grades.) Blackboards run across the front and on the right side, with the 26 letters in small and capital form mounted above the boards. A small bookcase full of books stands to the left of the door. A picture of George Washington and one of Abraham Lincoln hang on the wall, and a large, loudly-ticking clock hangs in the back. Adjacent on the west side are the two outhouses, one for boys on the north (with outer wall and cinders providing a urinal enclosing a two-seater), one for girls on the south (both customarily overturned on Halloween night). The metal flagpole stands up a slight knoll opposite the front door, with a well and pump just below it. The property is bounded on the north by the road, on the west and south by the Tipton fields and creek, and on the east by a relatively small grassy incline abutting the Judas property.

Sage (one-room) School

Existing records date from the year 1923-1924, with a total of 18 pupils and Mildred Frederick as teacher (earning $80 a month). All eight grades were under the tutelage of one teacher, and the peak enrollment was 24 (in 1949-50) (13 boys, 11 girls), with the low enrollment of 11 in 1951-52. The teachers, all female, were unquestionably a hardy lot, who probably did the best job they could under trying circumstances and with limited resources (with lowest pay at $50 a month and highest at $230). Some of them, to be sure, resembled Mr. Thomas Gradgrind in Charles Dickens' novel *Hard Times*—"A man of realities. A man of facts and calculations ... presented to the little pitchers before him, who were to be filled so full of facts ... He seemed a kind of cannon loaded to the muzzle with facts and prepared to blow them clean out of the regions of childhood at one discharge. He seemed a galvanizing apparatus, too, charged with a grim mechanical substitute for the tender young imaginations that were to be stormed away." And so at Sage the schoolmarms poured facts into the little pitchers, blew the innocents out of the regions of childhood, and stormed away at the tender young imaginations. From 1923 until 1952, there were 18 different teachers (one, Georgia Anderson, returned after her stint in 1944-45, to close out the school year of 1951-1952). Most of the teachers lasted only a year; a few had greater staying power. It was twenty-one years (1931-1952) from the time the first Kehl sibling entered Sage until its close (Melvin attended from 1931-1940; Maynard from 1932-1942, Johnnie from 1934-1944; Carolyn from 1937-1945; Mary from 1938-1947; Delmar from 1942-1950). The teachers during the Kehl tenure were:

Alma E. Smith (1931-1934) (became Alma Schmidt)
Mary Elizabeth Kilpatrick (1934-1935) (Known as "worst" and "cheapest" teacher—$50 per month. Kehl & Randecker kids quit a month before school was out for the summer because they allegedly weren't learning anything.)
Helen Schmidt Libberton (1935-1937) (Earned $60 per month. Kehl home quarantined for whooping cough)
Beatrice Gothard Halpin (1937-1938) (Earned $70 per month)
Ora Lou Kearnaghan Gelwicks (1937-1938) (Became sub when teacher got sick)
Velma N. Young (1938-1939)
Mae Strohecker (1939-1940) (Earned $85 per month. Reportedly a good teacher)
Alma Schmidt (1940-43) (Earned $85 per month. Reportedly a good teacher)
Virginia McCray (1943-44)
Georgia Anderson (1944-45, 51-52)
Florence Elliott (1945-49)
Alice Ward (1949-51)
Mrs. Paul R. Mackey, Georgia Anderson (1951-52)

The school was closed in the spring of 1952, consolidated with others, and country kids were required to attend school in Mt. Carroll.

Sage School Student Body (taken 1946, in schoolyard, with Judas farm buildings in background. Teacher: Florence Elliott. Mary—second row, 2nd from left; Del—second row, far right)

The County Superintendent of Schools for some years was Lawrence Brudi, who made regular yearly visits to Sage and other schools, spending several hours conferring with the teacher, walking up and down the aisles looking at students' work, and listening to classes "reciting."

During the last twenty-one years of Sage, these 85 pupils attended:

Adams, Junior
Bittner, George, Delores, David
Blair, Dale
Bowden, Ellsworth
Delp, Earl Jr.
Derrer, Ferne
Dewey, Daniel, Carol, Paul, Margaret
Dixon, Nancy, Robert, Donald
Ethridge, Edna Mae
Frederick, Virginia, Berniece, Floyd, Harvey, Sherman, Marie, Leo
Freeman, Alice
Gray, Wanda
Hansen, Delores
Howard, Floyd
Judas, Gene, Marvin, Marian
Kantlehner, Lester, Myrna

Kaufman, Ruby, Alfred
Kehl, Melvin, Maynard, Johnnie, Carolyn, Mary, Delmar
Knutzen, William
Lilly, Richard, Robert
Lynn, Alma Mae
Mader, Robert
Mason, William
McCall, Harlan
Misek, Annette, Jerry
Myers, Alta
Noble, Howard
Nowak, Ruth, Willard, Bobby, Lloyd, Melvin, Donna
Owens, Michael
Preston, Marijane, Nancy
Randecker, Wilma, Alice, Mabel, Dannie, Twila
Schubert, Gayle, Wayne, Lavonne, Jerry
Schmidt, Joan
Tipton, Frankie, John, Ethel, Sherman
Troxell, Kenneth
Wallmark, Carlton
Weeks, Mae, Tillie, Frank, Henry
Wubben, Harlan, Matilda, Dorothy, Gerald
Zink, Stanley, Juanita

When Mel and Maynard started school, they spoke as much German as English, and apparently the teacher was hard on them because of it. Maynard missed a lot of school because of illness: an eye infection and surgery on his ear when he was 6 or 8. The childhood diseases—whooping cough, chicken pox, and later measles and mumps—made the rounds. (Maynard missed more school when he had surgery on the mastoid in his ear and had to spend a week in the hospital at Freeport.) As they grew older, Mel, Maynard, and John often stayed home from school to help with the field work, missing out on much of the basics. They felt they had "better things" to do at home, and many times they hurried home to get there quicker so they could do things they liked to do. They attended "The School of Hard Knocks"—first the tests and then the lessons. Maynard and John have both said that one thing they might change would be to do better in school. (Each of the boys has been successful, but there's no telling what they might have done if they had received more formal education.)

Someone has said that anyone who enjoyed his or her schooldays was either a bully or a bore—the bully intimidating everyone, the bore wearying everyone. How many of those little "Sage" urchins, if we could interview them now, would say they actually enjoyed those years? For me, there were only intermittent times of enjoyment: the pungent smell of Big Chief notepads, freshly sharpened #3 pencils, white paste, and the excitement of new books for Reading or pristine workbooks for Spelling, the fascination of learning about exotic foreign lands in Geography—but those times were offset by those frustrating standardized word problem tests in Arithmetic ("Fred lives 15 miles from town, and Gregory lives 18 miles from town. If Fred leaves home at 8:00 and travels at 45 MPH and Gregory leaves at 8:30 and travels at 55 MPH, what time will each boy arrive in town?"), the frustration of sometimes going to the Recitation Bench feeling unprepared, or the embarrassment of having to do arithmetic problems on the board under the watchful eyes of the entire school.

Lester (Kantlehner) and I, being just two months apart in age, were classmates in the early years. There was a good bit of competition between us: he was good in arithmetic, which I soon came to dislike; I did especially well in reading, spelling, language/grammar, and geography. Before I was old enough to attend school, I recall being especially anxious to go, because I had learned to read books Carolyn brought home and I had gone along for a visit to school with my sisters and brothers. (My siblings later reported that I fell asleep and the teacher thought that would be a suitable time to pull a hair from my head so her science students could observe it under the microscope, but apparently I awoke and expressed my displeasure in no uncertain tones.) As noted above, I soon developed a dislike of Arithmetic and the routine of school in general, so after a few weeks of school, started faking illness in the morning until the others had gone to school; then I felt much better and had the entire day to play—or so I thought. Mother saw through my trickery and walked me to school. I recall the intense embarrassment (and even the lunch she packed for me—a scrambled egg sandwich on homemade bread). I had learned a different kind of lesson—and I settled in, never to play hooky again.

I developed a few friendships in grade school, including Lester, to some extent, and Bob Dixon, Bobby Nowak, and Frank Weeks. As I recall, the main topic of discussion on Mondays were the movies seen over the weekend (Roy Rogers, Gene Autry, Hopalong Cassidy, Royal Canadian Mounted Police, etc.), but since we Kehl kids weren't allowed to attend movies, I always felt "out of it" during those times. We also talked about radio programs we enjoyed (on that little Philco radio): "The Lone Ranger," "The Shadow," "Gangbusters," "Mr. District Attorney," "Fibber McGee and Molly," "The Great Gildersleeve," "Baby Snooks," "Meet Corlis Archer," "Oh Henry," etc. When I sent for a special revolver ring with a mounted gun and flint trigger which sent sparks that supposedly could be seen up to a mile away, the Dixon kids and I agreed that immediately after "The Lone Ranger" (5:30—6:00), I would go out into our field and flash the ring to test if they could see it from their place across the hills. I took a flashlight to first establish my presence and then flashed the ring numerous times. I was sure they must have seen it, but the next day at school, they said all they could see was the flashlight. (And like Ralphie in *The Christmas Story*, taken from Jean Shepherd's *In God We Trust: All Others Pay Cash*, I was anxious to receive the special secret code system, which included disappointing messages like "Drink your Ovaltine!" Another special offer was a highly touted attachment to "make your bicycle roar with the sound of a real motor"—a disappointing cardboard to rub against the spokes.)

Mary remembers that she and Carolyn walked home after school one day with Lavonne Schubert. Mrs. Schubert was making raisin-filled cookies and they got the recipe from her. (Mary says she still bakes them.) (See Chapter VII for the recipe.)

In 1941-42 the Judases, Schuberts, and Nowaks moved into the neighborhood. The kids were undisciplined and unruly, causing the teacher trouble and making it difficult for the other kids to learn. The teacher earned every nickel they paid her! When Wayne Schubert and "Fiddlepants" Randecker threatened to castrate Floyd Howard, the teacher sent them out to get a switch so she could paddle them. When I was in first grade, the "bully" was Wayne Schubert, who especially liked to pick on Lester. On one occasion, Wayne found some frog's eggs in the crick and made Lester eat them—or at least pushed them in his face. He was always messing up Lester's hair, pulling his pants down, or doing other such intimidating things. Wayne's sister Lavonne threatened to chase down every boy in school and kiss him. I recall thinking, "Hey, she's cute so that wouldn't be so bad; I won't run very hard." (Mae Weeks was also attractive to a little kid whose hormones were being activated—even in spite of her BO—and Nancy Preston was quite a knock-out in those tight sweaters she often wore!) (I recall Lavonne and several other girls whispering in the cloak room and giggling when they said I probably even didn't know what Kotex is, and I thought to myself, "What's the big deal about a Kodak; it's just a camera.") (I was madly "in love" with my

2nd grade teacher—Virginia McCray, to whom I wrote notes—and later with my 8th grade teacher—Alice Ward, for whom I veiled my feelings by being especially disagreeable.) Other pupils are memorable for various reasons—for example, Dannie Randecker (aka "Fiddlepants") for receiving a whipping in front of the whole school, Wayne and several other boys for putting a garter snake in the teacher's desk drawer, Leo Frederick for eating chalk, Willard Nowak for his love of sucking raw eggs, Lester for his tall tales of his sexual exploits.

The curriculum of Sage School was quite traditional and standard—in the words of the Mock Turtle in *Alice's Adventures in Wonderland* when asked what was taught in school: "Reeling and Writhing, of course, to begin with, and then the different branches of Arithmetic—Ambition, Distraction, Uglification, and Derision." That pretty much sums it up. Each school day began at 8:45 with the raising of the American flag by two pupils appointed for the week, with the rest of the schedule typically proceeding as follows:

Opening Exercises, including the Pledge of Allegiance.
Reading
Penmanship
Recess (10:30—11:00)
Arithmetic
Lunch (12:00—12:30)
Language, Grammar
Physiology, Health
Civics, Geography, or Science
Recess (2:05—2:20)
Spelling
Dismissal (3:30)

At the ringing of a bell, each grade would proceed to the Recitation Bench in the front, where each class sat and "recited"—questions were asked and (hopefully) answers given, discussion was conducted, and oral reading was sometimes done. Of course, everyone in the school could hear—and giggle—if mistakes were made, but all could also learn a great deal from other classes.

First grade included a strong emphasis on phonics and the "Dick and Jane" reading books ("See Dick. See Dick run. Run, Dick, run." Along with Sally and Spot). Earlier, according to Maynard, they read from charts—and the character was Sam. (I remember being quizzed on phonics letters, addition, and multiplication "facts" on flashcards by older students—Lavonne Schubert in particular.) I recall the "Reading Circle Books" and "The Weekly Reader." The sparse number of books on the "library" shelves ranged from 83 in 1923 to 220 in 1940 to 500 in 1950 (with some being damaged by fire in 1951, the total number dropping to 322 in 1952). I recall some of the books I read—for example, *Sid of Tarpaper Shack, The Little Shepherd of Kingdom Come, Treasure Island, Twenty Thousand Leagues Under the Sea.* Several of the teachers were good about reading books aloud (for example, Alice Ward, reading *Whispering Smith*). I still remember some of the stories in the books we used for Reading. One of my favorites was about the couple who seemed unhappy with their differing tasks, so they decided to do a role reversal. The wife went off to do the plowing and other farm work, while the husband stayed home to do the housecleaning, washing, and cooking. With somewhat of an early feminist twist, the wife seemed to do quite well, but it was disaster from the start for the husband, who flooded the house, burned the food, and was found by his wife hanging upside down from the chimney. In another story, a couple acquire a magic porridge pot, which cooks more and more and more porridge, until it flows out the doors and windows.

Mary says her greatest memory of Sage was how cold the room was in winter. "By the time the room got warm, it was time to go home! In the morning it was cold again!" I earned a bit of money by starting the fire in the furnace during my last few years, a job Dad got for me (he was on the school board for a number of years). That task was a real challenge, because, as Mary notes, it got very cold. I began with kindling and kerosene, then, at just the right time, began adding coal. Sometimes I had to start the fire several times and on a few occasions ran out of matches or kerosene and had to walk up to Judases and get some. One morning the furnace exploded and blew the door open, not only making a big mess but also leaving the room cold when the teacher arrived. (The Judases apparently kept a close eye on me because on one occasion they reported that I was taking library books off the shelves, which, of course, I was—but with no damage as I simply sat and read between shovels of coal while the fire got going.)

Most of the kids had some distance to walk to school—in rain, sleet, snow, and frigid weather—because there were no buses. Some, like the Fredericks and Kantlehners, had to walk across fields. Sometimes Art Kantlehner would pick Lester and Myrna up in the car—and would give us a ride home as well. I grew to like rainy or snowy days, because the attendance was often down and there was a more casual atmosphere. In winter, sometimes it grew dark by 2 o'clock, threatening snow or even a blizzard, and the teacher several times sent us home early. Usually in winter some kids brought sleds to school, riding down the hill past the schoolhouse, under the fence, and into the Tipton pasture beyond. Often two or three piled on for the ride, or we sat upright, steering with our feet. (On one occasion, Mary says she was forced to go, and made the corner past the schoolhouse, but hit the big tree beyond. Fortunately, she broke no bones but was sore for the Christmas program.) We all loved playing in the snow, making huge forts and having snowball fights, washing a favorite girl's face in the snow, rolling huge snowballs down the hill and blocking the outhouses (to the great displeasure of the teacher).

The two recesses and lunch were a favorite time for all. Sometimes we played softball, Andy-Andy-Over (throwing a ball over the roof, with the team trying to catch it and then run around and touching and capturing as many of the opposite team as possible), Frog-in-the-Well (played on the grassy hill, with one team holding individuals captive in the middle, while members of the other team attempted to run down and touch and "rescue" individuals—of course, targeting a favorite girl or boy), King of the Hill, Cowboys and Indians, Cops and Robbers, Blind Man's Bluff, Drop the Handkerchief, Rumor, etc. Mrs. Anderson's attempt at strictly supervised games (such as jumping rope) did not win much favor. (Once during one year I apparently had my feelings hurt during a recess and stood outside the school after recess, in full view of the entire school, with my right arm over my eyes, refusing to go back in. What an embarrassment that must have been for my siblings!)

During the afternoon recess on one Friday in late spring, Lester, Bobby Nowak, and I decided to go across the road into the Tipton woods. Lester produced a match and before we knew it he had started a fire that spread before we could stamp it out. Fortunately, Marv Judas soon saw it and came with his tractor to put it out. Needless to say, we were sent home forthwith, chagrined, and newly dubbed "the firebugs." The hardest part was facing my parents, trying to explain ("No, we *weren't smoking*!") and having to "face the music." But I distinctly remember Mother's understanding, her ready acceptance of my explanation, and especially her compassionate forgiveness.

Certainly one of the highlights of every school year was the Christmas program put on for the community, with usually standing room only.

There were songs, skits, plays, "pieces" or poems recited—the finale being a visit from Santa, a gift from the teacher (I still have my copy of Edward Eggleston's *The Hoosier Schoolmaster,* which I received from one of the teachers) and a bag for each pupil (with hard Christmas candy, nuts, and an orange). There were always hot dogs and a raffle for a goose (which we won on one occasion) and grab-bag gifts (one year Mary got a lemon squeezer, which she says she still has). The entire school would begin preparing for the program early in the fall, and the last week or so before would do little else. A poor performance would be a reflection on the teacher so it was a tense time; I recall the teacher one year breaking down and crying because students weren't learning their lines. I remember also being struck by how stern and gruff the teacher was with us and how affable and pleasant she suddenly became, just a few moments later, when guests started arriving.

One time, on the way home from a Christmas program, Art Kantlehner got stuck on the hill, driving his new Pontiac, but because it was during the war, he couldn't buy new tires. Maynard, taking Mom home from the program, roared right up the hill past him with his old Model-A. (I think he went back with the tractor to help him.)

Other holidays received less attention at school: Thanksgiving brought hectographed turkeys and pilgrims to color the day before vacation, and Easter brought eggs and bunnies to color. Valentine's Day, though, always meant a party with chocolate bunnies and eggs, along with heart-shaped candies stamped with terse little messages like "Be Mine," "Hug Me," "True Love," "Kiss Me Quick," "Love Always" and a big, decorated box into which we all put valentines for each other. The packets of generic valentines with trite messages were always rather disappointing, because they didn't say anything truly creative and passionate. I always tried to find just the right one for the special Object-Of-My-Eye (but then was always embarrassed when my Mom or sister would say, "You want this one for WHO?"—and I always looked for hidden passionate messages between the lines in the valentine I received from that special O-O-M-E.

The final day of school at the end of May was always celebrated with a family picnic, with each family bringing lots of food—fried chicken, ham, deviled eggs, potato salad, macaroni salad, baked beans, peas, corn, cole slaw, pickles and stuffed olives, topped off with various desserts (various kinds of homemade pies and cakes, cookies, jello), and sometimes the teacher brought ice cream. (I recall eating so much one year that I got sick—and lost it all.) Though we all looked forward to being out of school, this was always a nostalgic time because we wouldn't see most of our classmates for three months, after Labor Day—and a number of them, sadly, never again.

In a sense, Carolyn blazed the trail to high school, because she was the first of the Kehls to go on to that level, in 1945—and she should be commended for her persistence through difficult circumstances. We heard her formidable tales of Vera Fetterolf (Latin), Zella Corbett (Math), Izetta Robbe (Typing), Mr. Hodges (English), and others. When Mary graduated from eighth grade in 1947, Mother was sick, so Dad got papers signed so Mary could stay home and, for the next three years, she kept house, cooked, and fed the chickens. In 1950, when I graduated and was ready to enter high school, she went along to register as well, with no questions asked.

Mt. Carroll Community High School

As noted above, because I wasn't old enough to get a license, John took us to school and picked us up at the end of the day. When they were working in the field, sometimes it was rather late before he could make it to town, so we walked to the public library and did homework or read books while we waited. I loved being among the books, and resolved to read them all, beginning with "A," but soon came to realize that if I lived to be 100 and did nothing but read, I could never get through even the books in our little Carnegie Library! Following that epiphany, I had another—be selective, *Carpe diem* ("Seize the day"): not all the books in that library were *worth* reading, so concentrate on the best. I went through James Fenimore Cooper's *Leatherstocking Tales*, Jack London's western tales, Nathaniel Hawthorne's novels, some of Herman Melville's South Sea adventures such as *Typee* and *Omoo,* Steinbeck's novels, and Sinclair Lewis' novels, especially *Main Street,* about a small town (Gopher Prairie, Minnesota) that bore a striking resemblance to Mt. Carroll. (I also discovered Matthew Henry's *Commentary on the Bible* in a quiet upstairs corner, a wonderful treasure apparently unused or seldom used.)

High school was a considerably different world from Sage, and I remember being concerned about whether I had been adequately prepared to succeed, but Mother, demonstrating astute wisdom as she always did, reminded me that I had done my best in each of the eight grades and therefore would do well in 9-12. An initial impression was that there was an unspoken but clearly perceptible tension between town kids and country kids, the former attempting early to convey their notion that they were superior in every way. They had marked advantages, such as knowledge of "the ropes," having attended elementary school in the brick building adjacent to the three-story brick high school building. Many of them had played in the band, sung in the chorus, participated in athletics, and already knew most of the students and teachers. Another clear perception was that seriousness and studiousness, especially for boys, were not highly regarded, in fact, were a reason for some reproach.

The first day when we stepped out of the car and started down the sidewalk to the school door, I was met by six senior and several junior guys who escorted me and four other freshmen boys to waiting cars, blindfolded us, and drove us around and eventually south of town near the community of Wacker, and on a gravel road, took our shoes and socks, and dropped us off one by one. I, the first to be dropped off, started walking, fortunately in the right direction, and was soon picked up by a kind, gracious couple, who took me to the school door. This form of "initiation" hazing was countenanced by the administration and continued for some years thereafter. (I wish now that I had put up a fight, even though outnumbered!) (At the beginning of my last year of high school, as I drove my Model-A to pick up the mail, I came upon several freshmen walking barefoot on our gravel road, so I picked them up and took them to the paved highway, where they could catch a ride back to town. One of them was Harlan Brunner, who has expressed his appreciation several times years later.) Meanwhile, of course, I had missed all the orientation classes during the half-day of school, a great way to begin your high school career!

Early in the term, we took a battery of standardized tests. Shortly thereafter, the Principal, M. J. Siebert, called me to his office. Among other things, he asked if I had considered graduating in three years, which, he said, I could do by taking extra courses each year. His suggestion planted a seed, which grew to fruition three years later. (He was generally a good sort, in spite of the rumor that he was having an affair with his secretary, Anita Hurley Richards. Years later, seeing his name in the Phoenix newspaper, I gave him a call and thanked him for his service.)

Like Sage School, Mt. Carroll Community High School was small and modest. In my final year, 1952-53, there were 153 students (55 freshmen, 34 sophomores, 35 juniors, and 29 seniors) with 14 faculty members. All of the teachers at least had baccalaureate degrees (some from rather prestigious universities like the University of Chicago and William and Mary) and several had master's degrees (for example, John Condie, who taught English). During my three years, I had English I from Dorothy Huber, English II and III from John Condie (one of the finest teachers I've had anywhere), Latin I and II from Vera Fetterolf, Algebra, Geometry, and Advanced Algebra and Trigonometry from Zella Corbett, History from Augusta Stenquist, Social Studies from Robert Duffield (probably the worst teacher I've had anywhere at any time), General Science from Robert Allen, Biology from Andrew Hook, Beginning and Intermediate Typing and Shorthand from Izetta Robbe, Industrial Arts (required of all boys) from Charles Kirkpatrick, and Physical Education each year from Duffield and Hook. (I tried out for Chorus and Band but was not encouraged to continue; if I had attended elementary school in town, things might have been different.)

I learned most of my basic English grammar in Latin class, where we did conjugations and declensions each day on the board; if we did them correctly, we moved our chariots ahead in the "Chariot Race." Again there was a constant contest between town and country kids and, in this case, between female members and the lone male (me). I was also the only boy in the Shorthand (Gregg) class (which I took for the express purpose of facilitating note-taking for college). I always had Typing the first thing in the morning, and during the winter I would come in with stiff, cold fingers, which didn't adapt readily to easy, graceful movement and strokes. Miss Stenquist's History class was often a joke, with Jack Sipe making up fantastic news stories to share; everyone except the teacher seemed to realize his fabrications and were hardly able to stifle the giggles. Mary and I did Algebra and Geometry homework together, and I signed up for Advanced Algebra and Trigonometry because of scheduling conflicts and because I thought that taking something especially challenging would be good mental discipline. Miss Corbett would give us problems to work on in class while she sat at her desk and napped. Biology class was fascinating, especially with the dissecting of earthworms and frogs. (One evening when I was working on an assignment labeling an earthworm, Mel came out, looked over my shoulder, and asked if it was a jet engine.) Mary and I managed to convince Mr. Hook to show some of the Moody Institute of Science films, which drew the criticism of David Saidel, the school's one Jewish student. Duffield's Social Studies class was probably the biggest joke of all; ordinarily he spent class time either discussing the upcoming game or analyzing the last game, having students read aloud from the text, and assigning "busy-work" reports which he never read. In his PE classes (in good weather conducted down on the field near Point Rock Park, during foul weather in the gym), athletes on his teams were the favorites and recipients of his attention. We played touch football in the fall or sat listening to the World Series, basketball in winter, as well as tumbling and wrestling, softball or track and field in the spring. (When I outran several of his track stars in the 220, Hook asked if I wanted to "come out for track," which I did until transportation after practice became a problem.)

As a freshman I had to learn football and basketball from scratch ("Didn't you play touch football and basketball in junior high school?" "No, I attended a little, one-room country school with all eight grades— and we didn't have a football field or a gym.") (One winter afternoon during Duffield's PE class, when we were doing tumbling, I, along with Ed Kreppert, the Lutheran preacher's son, had some trouble executing the backward flip, but instead of helping, as he could easily have done, he remarked to a student-assistant, "Motor moron." My initial humiliation soon turned to seething anger. I thought of reporting this chain-smoking, beer-guzzling teacher to the Principal and School Board, but I let it go because I knew it would serve no good purpose anyway. I've used that nadir incident as motivation to rise above his low level.

For me, the highlight of all courses and teachers in high school was English II and III with John Condie. (I loved diagramming sentences, and he would sometimes ask my opinion about questionable cases.) Junior English has traditionally covered American literature; the widely used text, published by Harcourt, was *Adventures in American Literature* (the same text used four years later when I did my student teaching). (It's interesting to look today at the cover, a green thatch background with a photograph called "Desert Nocturne," with this inscription: "Taken at sunset in the Saguaro National Monument, located seventeen miles east of Tucson, Arizona. The giant cacti are known as saguaro and no two are exactly alike. A mature plant of 200 years may grow to a height of 50 feet and weigh from 6 to 10 tons." Admittedly, this typically Arizona photograph didn't mean as much 54 years ago: only God in His omniscient sovereignty could have said, "This beautiful state is where I have chosen for you to live and near this very spot your sons, daughters-in-law, and grandchildren will live!"

The selections in the book, giving an overview of American literature, resonated in a special way for me then and have ever since: short stories by Washington Irving, Nathaniel Hawthorne, O. Henry, Stephen Crane, Jack London, William Faulkner, John Steinbeck, James Thurber, Hamlin Garland, Frank Norris, Bret Harte, Mark Twain, and others, as well as poetry by Edward Taylor, William Cullen Bryant, Edgar Allan Poe, Sidney Lanier, Ralph Waldo Emerson, Walt Whitman, Emily Dickinson, E. A. Robinson, Robert Frost, Carl Sandburg, Vachel Lindsay, T. S. Eliot, Archibald MacLeish, and others, plus Thornton Wilder's *Our Town* (which was the play chosen to be produced by the school one year; Mr. Condie asked me to take a part in it, but because of transportation difficulties, I had to refuse the offer).

Mary and I studied vocabulary words together (using all kinds of mnemonics to help us remember them—for example, "say she ate" for *satiate*). I wrote a lengthy essay on "Death in American Literature," obviously too broad a subject to do justice to in a short paper, but I learned a great deal doing the research in the library. (I remember working on another writing assignment one weekend and getting up early on a Sunday morning to work on it before we went to church; this was the first time I had ever felt the sense of satisfaction and exhilaration at expressing something well in writing—a feeling confirmed when Mr. Condie read the essay aloud to the class.)

We weren't active socially in high school, not attending many games (only a few Christmas holiday tournament basketball games and a track meet or two) or even the Junior-Senior Prom. The school assemblies were sometimes memorable—including the showing of the movie *Les Miserables*, a one-man Shakespearean actor doing various sections of the plays, band and choral concerts (Marianne Ivy singing "The Wind's in the South Today"). I had no close friends in high school, though a few good acquaintances, such as Berkley Fetterolf, Ray Lucas, Freddie Coleman, Rich Rogers. I was anxious to be finished and off to college: bring on Edward Elgar and his "Pomp and Circumstance" march.

Carolyn had gone to Moody Bible Institute in 1950, where Mary was to go in 1954. After her graduation, Carolyn decided to get her B.A. and teaching certificate, so she and I went off together in September of 1953 to Bob Jones University in Greenville, South Carolina. We had to take the train to Chicago, change to The Empire Builder in the evening, ride all night, arrive in Atlanta the next morning, and change to Southern Railway to Greenville, another three-hour ride. At school we were able to see each other four days a week in chapel and sometimes met for a chat outside the Dining Common before dinner. We both got Work Loan Scholarships to help pay our expenses. (I waited tables one semester, then worked on the auditorium cleanup crew, getting up early each morning and also working Friday afternoons and evenings.) We were able to connect with other students from northwestern Illinois (in one case from Freeport) for a chartered bus, and later private car, to get home for Christmas and at the end of each year.

By working during the school year and during each summer (at the Green Giant Canning factory in Lanark, for Dr. Mershon on his farm in Pleasant Valley, and for painter Bob Davis), and with some help from Mother's egg money, I was able complete a double major in Biblical Studies and English, with a minor in History (including a correspondence course I took from the University of North Dakota in the summer). The following year, I attended the University of Wisconsin (Madison) to work on a Master's degree in English and Education (largely because of my admiration for the work of F. J. Hoffman, who taught modern American literature there and whose book *The Modern Novel in America* we had used in a class I had at BJU). During the following summer I worked at a bank in downtown Buffalo, N.Y., then went to Stamford, CT., where I taught

English for a year at the Roosevelt School at Shippan Point, a largely Jewish school endowed by the Roosevelts (for one outing we went to Manhattan, where we met Eleanor Roosevelt). I took two graduate courses at Fordham University in the Bronx, driving the 45-minute trip each Friday pm and Saturday morning. During the summer of 1960 while living and working in Elkins Park, PA, a suburb of Philadelphia, I took an evening course at the University of Pennsylvania.

In the fall of 1960, while working in Pasadena, CA, I took courses at Occidental College and the University of Southern California. One of my professors, Ronald Freeman, encouraged me to apply for a teaching-assistantship (teach two sections of freshman composition and take two graduate courses), which I did, enabling me to finish course work for the Ph.D., take the language exams (Latin and French), and the qualifying examinations. Meanwhile, of course, a major highlight: I met Wanda Thomas, and we were married in August of 1963. We lived one year in Pasadena and one in Alhambra, while I studied for and took the exams, then began work on the dissertation ("The Dialectics of Reality in the Fiction of Robert Penn Warren"; Warren was a gracious Southern gentleman with whom I carried on an interesting correspondence). I defended the dissertation in 1967 and officially received the Ph.D. This academic career might suggest to some a case of education beyond intelligence, but I hope I can say with Mark Twain, "I have never let my schooling interfere with my education."

VII. Flavor of a Family: Proof of the Pudding Is in the Eating

"You shall eat of the fruit of the labor of your hands;
you shall be happy, and it shall be well with you."
(Psalm 128:2)

"Every man who eats and drinks sees good in all his
labor—it is the gift of God." (Ecclesiastes 3:13)

"She provides her supplies in the summer, and gathers
her food in the harvest." (Proverbs 6:8)

"'You must sit down,' says Love, 'and taste my meat.' So
I did sit and eat." (George Herbert, "Love")

"The bread I break with you is more than bread."
(Conrad Aiken)

"Let your boat of life be light, packed with only what
you need—a homely home and simple pleasures, one
or two friends, with the name, someone to love and
someone to love you, a cat, a dog… enough to eat and
enough to wear…"
(Jerome K. Jerome, *Three Men in a Boat*)

"Strange to see how a good dinner and feasting
reconciles everybody." (Samuel Pepys, *Diary*)

"Tell me what you eat, and I shall tell you what you are."
(Anthelme Brillat-Savarin, *The Physiology of Taste*)

How often have we heard it said that "you are what you eat," maybe a folk version of the Frenchman's challenge, "Tell me what you eat, and I shall tell you what you are" (Anthelme Brillat-Savarin, 1825)? If the proof—or measure—of **being** is in the **eating**, the Kehl family could be said to have fared quite well, because we always ate well on the farm—or, as it might have been expressed then, we ate "high on the hog," not in the sense that we were affluent but in the sense that we always had a variety of nutritious, delicious food—and plenty of it, although we kids probably didn't appreciate it as we should have at the time.

It must have been especially satisfying to our parents that life on the farm was quite self-sustaining, necessarily so: we raised almost everything we needed (and then some), buying only such staples as flour, sugar, salt, pepper and other herbs and spices (cinnamon, cloves, nutmeg, ginger, paprika, allspice, turmeric), baking soda, yeast, mustard, vinegar, vanilla, coffee, tea. When some of those items were rationed during the war years, we skimped or did without, but none of us remember feeling "deprived." Mother was a superb household manager and excellent cook. Beef cows provided ample milk for drinking and cooking. (I remember that on one occasion in the milk barn, one of my brothers, John, I believe, squirted milk into my mouth directly from the udder source. Wouldn't Louis Pasteur have been appalled? There but for the grace of God go the fermentative bacteria!). Contented cows also provided rich cream (simply skimmed off the top or processed with a crank cream-separator), butter made in a rotating, arm-powered churn and stowed in the deep "arch cellar" for refrigeration during summer, rich buttermilk (for those who liked it), cottage cheese, and, of course, beef. Hogs—the Spotted Poland China variety—provided our pork, and chickens supplied our eggs, along with fried, roasted, or boiled feasts and hearty broth for soup.

We seldom, almost never, bought bread, which Mother baked as needed, or any meat, though sometimes ring baloney and cheese, maybe lemons for lemonade (on the 4th of July or other special occasions). (I recall envying other kids at school who brought lunches of sandwiches made with "baker's bread" or "store-bought bread" and "minced ham," although I felt no envy for the lard sandwiches one family's kids sometimes had.) When Mother made biscuits, the round pan she used held ten. Sometimes someone would come by and snitch one out and pinch them together, thinking she wouldn't know, but she did. She always counted how many she put in the pan to bake; she couldn't be fooled! And her baking-powder biscuits were popular with everyone.

Baking Powder Biscuits
2 cups flour
4 teaspoons baking powder
½ teaspoon salt
4 tablespoons shortening
¾ cup milk (can be ½ water)
Sift together flour, baking powder and salt. Add shortening and mix in with fork. Add milk to make soft dough. Turn out on floured board and toss lightly until outside looks smooth. Roll ½ inch thick. Cut with floured cutter. Place on greased pan. Bake in oven 475 degrees for about 12 minutes.

Also receiving high acclaim were her homemade doughnuts.

Doughnuts (Donuts)
1 cup sugar
2 eggs
1 teaspoon salt
1 teaspoon lard
½ teaspoon orange (or other) extract
1½ cup milk
2 teaspoons baking powder
½ teaspoon cinnamon
½ teaspoon nutmeg
¼ teaspoon ginger
4 ¾ cups flour
3 pounds fat for frying
½ cup powdered sugar (for top)
Beat eggs slightly. Add sugar, salt, and lard. Blend well. Add extract, flour sifted with dry ingredients, and milk. Mix well. If necessary, add enough more flour to handle, but keep dough as soft as possible. Roll ½ inch thick. Cut with floured cutter. Heat fat in deep kettle. Cook 5-6 doughnuts at a time for 3-4 minutes. If turned frequently during cooking, they are less likely to crack badly. Drain on absorbent paper and sprinkle with powdered sugar.

It should be remembered that Mother cooked, baked, canned fruits and vegetables—all on that wood-burning Majestic cook stove! What an amazing, enterprising, multi-talented woman she was!

Butchering days were major annual events—beef in the fall, often between Christmas and the New Year, hogs in spring, usually March. Dad's expertise at butchering was widely known, so he had numerous requests every year to help the neighbors with theirs. The cow or hog was suspended from a limb of the "Butcher Tree." It was skinned, eviscerated, and sectioned to be cut up on the kitchen table. Mother did most of the cutting, smoking, and canning of the meat and supervised the entire methodical process that wasted nothing (it was said that they used everything but the moo and the squeal). Because we didn't have electricity, Mother canned one hind quarter, which could be used for "rivel soup" or just heated and the broth used for gravy.

Rivel Soup
3 cups flour
2 eggs
½ cup water
1 large beaten egg
1 cup flour
¼ teaspoon salt
Mix together by hand to form small rivels or pieces. Stir into hot broth.

One hind quarter was used for sausage in the spring, when the pigs were butchered. She sold the beef hide for a good price, scaled the hog hides and scraped off the bristles, cooked the rinds and liver together and made delicious liverwurst, a favorite breakfast treat. She fried the brains (also delicious with eggs for breakfast, accompanied by recurring jokes about increasing our IQs), used the ears and head meat for making head cheese (not so popular with some of us), boiled the pig's feet—a delicacy—scraped and cleaned the beef tongue for pickling—all gourmet quality, though we didn't realize it at the time. Mother and Dad laboriously purged, cleaned, and scraped the pork intestines for sausage casings, using a sausage stuffer to make the sausage and also to press the lard (the pervasive smell that permeated the house made those times of "rendering out the lard" unpleasant ones for us kids), to be used for shortening in cakes, pies, and other cooking. (In those days we had never heard of cholesterol, triglycerides, saturated fats, or any such formidable terms. We had fried foods constantly and were required to eat all the fat on our meat, wasting nothing. Yet Dad lived to age 95, Aunt Ella to 94, Aunt Lula to 93, and several other aunts well into their 80's.) When the pigs were butchered, Mother "fried down" a lot of the meat and "sugar-cured" the hams and shoulders. (The Rockford relatives especially liked the "fried-down" meat when they came to visit.) The sausage was hung in the smokehouse to be smoked, later to be fried and packed in crocks with lard to keep it.

If the beef and pork were all gone or if we wanted more variety, we sometimes had rabbit, squirrel, pheasant, (even pigeons on occasion), sometimes fresh fish (usually carp) from Plum River. (I remember on one occasion going with Dad, Maynard, and John to fish in the river, my job being to stay on the bank, watch for the Game Warden, and sound a warning if he appeared, while they seined for fish or tried spearing them. Maynard was especially skilled at catching fish by hand avoiding bullheads). Sitting with a hook, line, and sinker was decidedly not the preferred method, except for Uncle Chris. (During that time, I didn't care much for fish because once I got a bone stuck in my throat and was panicking until Mother gave me a piece of bread to get it on down my throat.) On one occasion, Mother roasted a coon and invited the neighbors to enjoy the delicacy with us (parboiling it first to get rid of the smell), featuring, as I recall, freshly baked gingerbread topped off with whipped cream for dessert. Of course, we always had plenty of chicken, every which way but raw—fried, roasted, boiled, or in soup with Mother's homemade noodles. No one could make noodles as she did.

Noodles
4 cups flour
6 eggs
½ cup water (more or less)
1 teaspoon salt
Mix together. Roll into thin sheet. Dry thoroughly. Roll into a roll, then cut into thin strips.

She rolled the dough and hung it on cloth-covered backs of chairs to dry by the stove; when they were dry she rolled them up and cut them expertly in even pieces, her left hand moving along measuring the width, her right hand cutting in rhythm. She also made excellent fried chicken (much superior to any the Colonel, of course unknown then, was to produce or even imagine). With our large family, a single chicken, which she skillfully beheaded with a corn knife on a chopping block, didn't go very far. Which piece you got depended on where you were sitting at the table. The "white meat," called "cat meat" by the boys, was not as favored as the dark meat. Dad loved the neck, and the back was Mother's, so we all knew to pass those by.

Mother always had a huge vegetable garden in one of five different locations, as noted above. The annual gardening began in early spring with Dad or one of the boys plowing the ground and preparing it for planting. As soon as the frost was out of the ground, Mother would say, "It's time to scratch in a little lettuce"—and scratch she did! Not only did we live "high on the hog," we lived "off the fat of the land."

Besides lettuce, she raised cabbage, radishes (both red and white), Swiss chard, Brussels sprouts (sounds downright cosmopolitan), cauliflower, eggplant, spinach, endive, turnips, parsnips, sweet potatoes (yams?), carrots, asparagus (I called it "sparrow guts") celery, tomatoes, onions, beets, dill, potatoes, sweet corn, peas, green beans, lima beans, navy beans, cucumbers, summer squash, acorn squash, pumpkins, rhubarb, sometimes kohlrabi, sometimes horseradish. Tomato plants had to be set out, with water carried in a five-gallon bucket—but all worth it. (I recall coming home from school, changing clothes, getting a big slice of homemade bread, spread with homemade butter and tomato preserves or apple butter, then hearing Mother say, "Kids, let's go out and hoe a little while." Sometimes we groaned, but we all took justifiable pride in an immaculate, weed-free garden!)

Digging potatoes was another big chore, with Dad or one of the boys plowing them out with the tractor, and three or four of us coming behind picking them up, brushing off the dirt, and putting them in gunny-sacks for storage in a cellar bin. Sometime later, sitting in the cellar bin sprouting potatoes is another vivid memory. (I also recall coming home from school, getting a butcher knife, going back to the pasture garden, selecting a muskmelon and/or watermelon, and sitting down to enjoy the savory snack; if the first wasn't quite to my liking, I threw it over the fence to the cows and got another, maybe another, maybe yet another. I'm ashamed of my wastefulness as I think of it now, but the cows liked it. Or I'd sometimes take a salt shaker or salt in wax paper and "pig out" on those big red juicy tomatoes right from the vine!)

We also had a huge strawberry patch, carefully tended with straw between the rows. The berries were plentiful all season long. We got tired of stooping over to pick them and by the end of the season, having had them usually twice a day—strawberries and cream, strawberry custard pie, strawberry "lid" crust pie, strawberry cobbler, and, of course, strawberries alfresco—most of us were "fed out" on them (until we had canned ones in the middle of winter or, later, frozen strawberries with ice cream).

We were fortunate to have such a variety of fresh vegetables and fruit so readily available. We had both blue and red raspberries growing adjacent to the orchard and a blackberry patch in the garden by the granary. Mother canned blue raspberries and blackberries, which we enjoyed eating with *fettdotshures* (rather like the Spanish *sopopilla*). Mother usually grew huckleberries for pie (my all-time favorite, followed by banana cream and coconut cream) and ground cherries (each yellow, seed-clustered cherry in its own little paper bag—Isn't the Lord's creation amazing?) (also excellent for jam). Mother made delicious berry-custard pies, as well as berry crust pies. Mary and I recall the time the Rev. Birdsall was driving past our house when a storm came up, and he stopped in, so Mother invited him to have dinner (mid-day meal) with us. He expressed his surprise that we ate two whole pies at one meal (each cut in fourths, the extra piece sometimes being the object of some controversy).

The orchard had three of four different kinds of apples, the season commencing in September with the Golden Transparent (I wonder how many stomach aches I endured from eating raw apples), also one pear tree, a peach tree (that never did very well), a cherry tree (the birds got most of the fruit), a mulberry tree down in the hog pasture (wonderful to climb and sit on a branch picking berries with both hands and gobbling them up), and elderberries (good for jam). Mother would often cut up the apples, put them in a bag, and hang them beside the stove or on the back of the pantry door to dry for making pies in winter. Apple dumplings were also a huge favorite, as well as "Apple Cholat," Dad's favorite dessert (or was it the cheese pie?).

Apfel Cholat
1½ cups sugar
½ cup lard
3 eggs
1½ cups milk
3 teaspoons baking powder
3 cups flour

Mix this together like for a cake. Mixing bowl of apples sliced like for apple pie. Mix apples and dough together, place in loaf pan, add sour cream on top and sprinkle sugar on top. Bake until apples are soft.

Apple Dumplings
Use the baking powder biscuit dough (q.v.).
Add ¼ cup sugar. Do not put in as much milk.
Cut in squares in which an apple is placed.
Add sugar and cinnamon.

Apple Butter
Apples
Water
½ as much sugar as apples
Cinnamon and cloves (to taste)
Boil together until thick.

Of course, we seldom had much of the more exotic fruit like bananas, oranges, grapefruit, or pomegranates, but both red and blue plums grew wild in various places, as well as gooseberries, wild strawberries, raspberries, blackberries, and "May apples" in the woods. We had a Concord grape arbor along the north side of the lane; with so many grapes we got tired of having them for school lunches. (They made especially delicious grape juice.) The folks would ordinarily get a lug of Michigan or Georgia peaches (about $3 a bushel) which Mother used for pies, cobbler, and for canning (although a goodly number of them never made it to the pan or the jar). In addition, the folks often got a crate of prunes or raisins (in 4-pound bags) (which were especially tasty for raiding). Mother often made (cottage) cheese pie, with raisins and/or orange extract, another favorite dessert of Dad's.

Cheese Pie
4 cups cottage cheese
2 cups sugar
4 eggs
2 tablespoons flour
1 cup cream (or more)
½ cup raisins or orange flavor
Pour in unbaked pie shell. Bake until firm.

She also made delicious raisin meringue pie.

Raisin Meringue Pie
Baked pie shell
½ cup sugar
2/3 cup seeded raisins
1½ cup water
1 2/3 cup cream
1/8 teaspoon salt
3 egg yolks
3 tablespoons cornstarch
½ teaspoon vanilla
3 egg whites
2 tablespoons powdered sugar
Put sugar, raisins and water in pan and bring it to a boil. Cook 5 minutes. Mix cornstarch with a little teaspoon milk. Add beaten egg yolks, salt and cream. Add to raisin mixture. Cook until thick. Add vanilla. Pour into baked pie shell. Make meringue of egg whites beaten until stiff but moist. Add 3 tablespoons sugar. Bake in slow oven (300 degrees) for ½ hour or until brown.

Mother also canned lots of peas, beans, tomatoes (and juice), and corn, and Mary remembers having cabbage, carrots, and winter radishes stored in the "arch cellar." Mother made cabbage into sauerkraut—placed in large crocks with plates upside down, weighed down with heavy rocks. Sauerkraut and dumplings, with ribs cooked in the kraut, was Dad's favorite meal. Some of us preferred *spatsa* to the dumplings, but Mother's dumplings were justifiably touted as being "light as a feather."

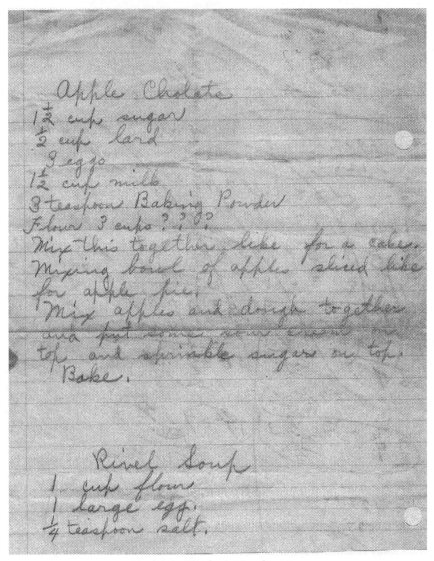

Recipe in Mother's Handwriting

For breakfast, Mother often made pancakes (Dad especially liked buckwheat pancakes), which we ate with lots of butter, sorghum, maple syrup, or honey. Or we often had oatmeal, Ralston, fried or scrambled eggs with homemade liverwurst or sausage. Sometimes we had cornflakes (Kelloggs or Sunnyfield) or another cereal originally called Cheeri-Oats (in 1941). For snacks we kids sometimes ate raw, dry oatmeal—in a cup with a spoon, which was really quite tasty.

The mid-day meal was always called "dinner," no little, skimpy lunch but a substantial meal to carry the men through the long afternoons of hard work in the field. Meat, potatoes and gravy, and a vegetable, plus pie or cake for dessert were common. School lunches often included a fried-egg or scrambled-egg sandwich on homemade bread, or bread and homemade jelly or jam. Other school lunch items were hard-boiled eggs, soup left over from the evening before (for example, potato soup, noodle soup, macaroni soup) carried in a thermos bottle, or macaroni with tomatoes (my special favorite) carried in a Mason jar. Sometimes there was a chicken leg or rabbit or squirrel meat, canned peaches, apples, pears, or grapes in season. Mother, and often Mary, made big batches of cookies—snickerdoodles (my favorite), chocolate chip, oatmeal-raisin, cocoanut, chocolate, gingersnaps, raisin-filled—so they were often part of the school lunches. (Maynard remembers eating lunch with Sherman and Harvey Frederick, who sometimes had rice chocolate cookies, dipped in chocolate with a marshmallow and half a walnut on top. He remembers Sherm loving to snitch the nut from Harvey's cookies.)

Raisin-Filled Cookies (Mrs. Roy Schubert)
2 cups sugar
2 eggs
1 cup lard
Pinch of salt
1 teaspoon vanilla
½ teaspoon soda
1 cup sour cream
1 teaspoon baking powder
Flour enough to roll thin (about 5 cups)
Raisin filling same as for pie (about 1 lb. box). Cook 2½ cups raisins, water. Add ¾ cup sugar. 2 tablespoons flour. Cook until thick. Roll the dough rather thin. Cut with a cookie cutter. Place one cookie on a baking sheet. Place spoonful of raisin filling on top, then place another cookie on top and seal edges. Bake in moderate oven until firm. Do not over-bake. Makes about 4 dozen medium size cookies.

Ginger Cookies (Aunt Cora)
1 cup sugar
1 cup shortening
2 eggs

½ cup molasses (Br'er Rabbit)
½ teaspoon cloves
½ teaspoon cinnamon
½ teaspoon ginger
1 level teaspoon soda
¼ teaspoon salt
3 cups flour

Roll into narrow rolls and flatten out on greased cookie sheet. Put water on the top and sprinkle with sugar. When baked, cut across angle.

The evening meal—supper—often consisted of leftovers from "dinner." Boiled potatoes left over from "dinner" became sliced fried potatoes, creamed potatoes, potato salad, or scalloped potatoes for supper.

Skillet Creamed Potatoes
3-4 tablespoons bacon drippings
6 cups dried cooked potatoes
½ cup chopped green onions
Salt and pepper, to taste
3 tablespoons flour
1½ cups milk

Heat drippings in skillet. Add potatoes and onions. Stir until heated through. Sprinkle with salt and pepper. Add flour. Stir well. Add milk and cook until thickened. Cool down fairly well.

Scalloped Potatoes
1 quart sliced raw potatoes
2 cups scalded milk
4 tablespoons butter
3 tablespoons flour
1 teaspoon pepper

Cover bottom of a buttered dish with a layer of potatoes. Sprinkle with salt, pepper, and dab of butter plus a dredge of flour. Repeat. Pour over milk. Bake at 350 degrees for 45-50 minutes.

Prize Salad Dressing (for potato salad)
1 well-beaten egg
6 level tablespoons sugar
5 tablespoons flour

Salt

1 cup milk

Cook until thickened. Add ½ cup vinegar.

A roast might become stew; fried chicken may be served cold; sauerkraut warmed over had an even better flavor. We usually had milk or Kool-Aid to drink (from the variously, individually flavored packs or the McNess bottles of flavoring), no soda or "pop" as it was called then (except for homemade root beer on several occasions). (The popularity of iced-tea came later. I remember first drinking it—and loving it—with dinner at Maders while we were baling hay there.) There was always a tasty dessert of pie, cake, or cookies and, in winter when there was ice available from the horse tank, sometimes homemade ice cream—the always popular vanilla or strawberry or peach—"ripening" in a snowbank until just the right moment.

Sunday meals broke the routine somewhat—usually a quick breakfast of cereal before church, then often "rivel" soup for "dinner," and, in late afternoon, after the adult naps and Mother's letter-writing and reading, popcorn served in a huge dishpan (with Dad's ground up and served with milk in a bowl, to be eaten with a spoon), often followed by popcorn balls, with enough left over for school lunches on Monday. Usually we listened to Charles Fuller's "Old Fashioned Revival Hour" and Billy Graham's "Hour of Decision" as we munched on popcorn, feeding both our bodies and our souls.

Much of the food on the farm was seasonal. When fresh, rich soup-bones were available after butchering beef, we had a variety of soups as the main course—noodle, rivel, macaroni, carrot, navy bean, vegetable—along with fresh-baked bread or biscuits. One year Mother made a delicious vegetable soup with a tomato base, but when several became ill, the soup was blamed (probably unjustly: the illness was likely the flu) and it was summarily thrown out.

During late spring, throughout summer, and in early fall, we enjoyed fresh vegetables from the garden and fruit from the orchard and berry patches. God, in His sovereign wisdom, seemed to space the various fruit and vegetable harvests to our best advantage. (Working down at Maynard's farm while baling hay, I recall the great meals Bernice fixed. She was such a great cook. I especially loved her chili, made with rice and kidney beans.)

Chili con Carne (Bernice)
2 tablespoons fat
1 small onion
1 pound ground beef
1 teaspoon salt
1 can tomatoes (4 cups)
1 can red kidney beans (2 cups)
1 cup (uncooked) rice
Chili powder and pepper (to taste)
Brown beef and onion in fat. Cook rice in water. Add to beef and remaining ingredients. Simmer until all is well blended.

Creative and enterprising as Mother was, she made good use even of things not grown in the garden. For example, she sometimes cooked what we called "weeds" (docks, plain not curly, that grew wild out in the pasture down below the cattle shed) cooked with potatoes, mashed and thickened with flour, eaten with early green onions. She also made something called *mauldresher*, onion-and-bread-filling in tucked noodle dough (which tasted much better than it sounds). A favorite of everyone in the family were the wild morel mushrooms, resembling a sponge on a stalk, that grew around trees down on the sand-bank hill. (What a great time Carolyn, Mary, and I used to have looking for them in the spring!) After thoroughly cleaning and washing them, Mother fried them in butter. How tasty they were!

During the long, often cold and desolate, winters, we enjoyed all the canned foods Mother had stored in the "arch cellar"—peas, corn, beets, green beans, tomatoes, as well as peaches, pears, raspberries, blackberries, strawberries, huckleberries (for pie), along with all the jellies, jams, and preserves she put away.

Canned Beans
Boil green beans in water and salt until tender. Drain and add:
4 cups vinegar
4 cups water
2 teaspoons salt
1 teaspoon pepper
1 teaspoon cinnamon
2 cups sugar
Heat beans thoroughly and put in jars. Seal (When opened, heat and add onions.)

Especially tasty were the variety of pickles she made—dill, bread-and-butter pickles, canned beat pickles, watermelon pickles, apple pickles, ripe cucumber pickles, sliced cucumber pickles, mixed pickles (also called Chow-Chow), and mustard pickles (the favorite of Maynard and me. I would often sneak into the pantry, where they were kept in one-gallon crocks, and snitch some)

Mustard Pickles
1 pint (2 cups) vinegar
2 tablespoons salt
2 tablespoons dry mustard
2 tablespoons sugar
Mix and pour over small-to-medium size cucumbers. Cover in crock until seasoned through.

Ripe Cucumber Pickles
Pare and remove seeds from ripe cucumbers. Cut into strips. Cover with salt and let stand overnight. In the morning drain and rinse until salt is removed. Prepare syrup:
1 quart vinegar
2 cups sugar
2 tablespoons broken-stick cinnamon
1 teaspoon whole cloves
1 teaspoon allspice
1 teaspoon salt
Cook cucumbers in it until they are clear and transparent. Pack in jars. Cover with hot syrup and seal.

Canned Beet Pickles
1 pail beets
4½ cups vinegar
4 tablespoons salt
1 teaspoon pepper
1½ cups sugar
4 cups water
Cook and peal beets. Make syrup of remaining ingredients. Place all in jars and seal. Makes 6-7 quarts.

When the beets were all gone, Mother often put hard-boiled eggs in the brine to soak, resulting in delicious, flavorful pink eggs.

Mixed Pickles (or Chow-Chow)
1 quart onions
1 quart big cucumbers, sliced
1 quart small cucumbers
1 quart green tomatoes, sliced
1 large head of cabbage, sliced
Optional: 1 head of cauliflower, 4 small sweet peppers
Mix together and cover with brine of 1 gallon water and 1 cup salt. Soak for 4 hours. Set on fire in the same brine. Let it scald but do not cook. Drain and add dressing:
4 tablespoons dry mustard
1 teaspoon turmeric powder
1 cup flour
3 cups sugar
2 quarts vinegar
Mix mustard, turmeric and flour with a little vinegar. Pour in sugar and rest of vinegar. Cook until thick. Pour over pickles and mix. Put in jars and seal.

Holidays also brought special foods and dishes that formed much-appreciated traditions. For Thanksgiving we enjoyed roasted duck or goose, fried or roasted chicken, sometimes pheasant, along with all the trimmings, including Mother's special onion-based dressing/stuffing, mashed potatoes and gravy, several vegetables, freshly baked bread or biscuits, different kinds of pickles, all topped off (ordinarily) with pumpkin pie (from real pumpkins, not from a can), mincemeat pie, or raisin pie and whipped cream.

Pumpkin Pie
2 cups pumpkin
1 1/3 cups sugar
2 tablespoons flour
3 cups milk
2 eggs
1/8 teaspoon ginger
1 teaspoon cinnamon

¼ teaspoon nutmeg

1/8 teaspoon cloves

1/8 teaspoon allspice

Mix all ingredients together and place in unbaked pie shell. Bake until firm.

Mincemeat Pie (Bernice?)

1 pound cooked lean beef

2 cups brown sugar

1 cup suet

1 pound raisins

1 pound currants

2 cups cider

1 pound tart apples

½ teaspoon cinnamon, nutmeg, mace, and cloves

1 teaspoon salt

2 cups grape or cherry juice, meat broth

Cook until almost tender. Cool. Chop apples, suet, and beef. Add remaining ingredients, allowing just enough meat broth to cover. Simmer until the apples are tender. Seal at once in hot jars.

Christmastime brought other food traditions, including various candies, such as fudge with homegrown and freshly cracked walnuts or hickory nuts (Dad was the expert nut-cracker; he know just how to hit the shell in just the right place so the nutmeat could be picked out in a single piece. I remember sitting in the "woodbox," cracking nuts, the shells falling where they may), divinity fudge, sometimes taffy, and coconut peaks (made, if you can believe it, with mashed potatoes).

Coconut Peaks

¾ cups cold mashed potatoes

4 cups powdered sugar

4 cups coconut

1½ teaspoons vanilla

1/8 teaspoon salt

4 squares of milk chocolate

Blend all ingredients except chocolate. Form into peaks on greased surface. Dry uncovered for 20 minutes. Melt chocolate. Dip bases of each in chocolate. Let stand on wax paper until firm. Makes 2½ pounds.

There were also a variety of Christmas cookies, for example, sugar cookies cut in the shapes of seasonal icons and decorated—snowmen, angels, Santa with pack, stars, bells. For Easter, we usually had Mother's much-loved *kuchen* (a coffee cake made with bread dough, flattened out and greased with sugar and cinnamon on top) and a wild, sour red-plum pudding with cream sauce in a crust (called "pluma-stuff," a favorite of all, but especially John). Independence Day food traditions included, as I recall, lemonade made from real lemons and sharp cheddar cheese on crackers.

There was always a special cake—or sometimes pie—for birthdays. Favorites were angel food, devil's food, plain chocolate, or hickory nut cake.

Devil's Food Cake
½ cup cocoa
2 teaspoons soda
½ cup boiling water
Mix together and let stand while mixing.
1¾ cup sugar
¾ cup butter
Add cocoa mixture
¾ cup sour milk
2½ cups flour
Fold in 2 beaten egg whites.

Chocolate Cake
½ cup sugar
2 squares chocolate (or 3)
1 cup milk
Boil 5 minutes and cool.
½ cup shortening
1 cup sugar
2 eggs
2 cups flour
2 teaspoons soda (dissolved in 3 tablespoons hot water)
½ cup milk
1 teaspoon vanilla
1 teaspoon salt
Cream sugar and shortening well. Add chocolate mixture. Add eggs. Sift flour and salt. Add soda and water, vanilla. Bake in maximum oven.

Nut Cake

1 cup sugar
½ cup butter
½ cup milk
¾ cup chopped nuts
1¾ cup flour
2 teaspoons baking powder
1 teaspoon vanilla
Whites of 3 eggs

Cream butter and add sugar and cream until light. Add the flour and milk alternately with the baking powder and a pinch of salt. Lastly, add the egg whites. Put ½ cup chopped nuts in the icing.

Other events or gatherings brought special culinary feasts. A notable example, mentioned above, was threshing, when four or five different neighbors would gather together to help each other, the women coming along to help prepare special feasts for dinner. There were usually three kinds of meat—surely fried chicken, ham, maybe beef—,three or four vegetables—usually corn, green beans, maybe baked beans, maybe lima beans, peas, maybe squash—, maybe hominy, maybe spaghetti (from a can), maybe a casserole or two, plus pickles and olives, and surely homemade bread or biscuits, plus jello, two kinds of pie, maybe a cake or two, and cookies. If anyone ever left the table hungry, it was his own fault. Such feasts gave rise to the expression "enough food for threshers."

Family reunions were other occasions for feasts, potlucks to which each family contributed their best and favorite dishes. Aunt Emma's macaroni salad was a memorable dish, as well as Aunt Lula's Cherry Crisp Pie, her Rhubarb Cream Pie, her Chocolate Pudding, and her Cranberry Salad, Mrs. (Roy) Schubert's Raisin-Filled cookies, Aunt Ella's Marshmallow Salad and her Carrot Salad, Aunt Cora's Ginger cookies, Aunt Muriel's Devil's Food Cake, Mother's Sour Cream Chocolate Cake, to mention only a few. Reunion dinners were usually topped off with an ample supply of delicious Meadow Gold ice cream.

All of us had our own tastes and peculiarities of preference and dislike. Dad's favorite meal was sauerkraut, dumplings, and ribs cooked in the kraut (he hated cooked tomatoes), with Apfel Cholat or Cheese Pie for dessert. Mel loved Limburger cheese, the more odiferous the better, and was especially fond of Sour Cream Chocolate Cake. Neither he nor Maynard or John liked scrambled eggs (called "stinkin' eggs") or cottage cheese. Maynard loved mustard pickles, raw onions; he had the habit of smelling everything before he would eat; he hated butter and anything cooked or baked with butter (and always asked if there was butter in the cake or pie). John was especially fond of the "pluma stuff" Mother made at Easter time. Carolyn and Mary seemed to like just about everything, with no memorable complaints. I never cared much for sauerkraut and dumplings and especially disliked the meat cooked in the kraut. As a little kid I loved acorn squash, but after an illness, even the smell of it (along with sweet potatoes and yams) turned my stomach.

So-called "comfort" or "soul" foods in our family were mashed potatoes and gravy, one of the homemade soups (especially rivel or noodle), or homemade bread or biscuits. (Numbers of times when I was sick, I remember asking for "Granma soup," which was bread broken up in a little hot water, with added milk, salt and pepper. And once when Mary was sick and was asked what she might like, she said, "I *could* eat a banana.")

We never splurged on gourmet foods, even when they might be available at the local A & P, Nobles' Red & White, or Royal Blue. I never tasted grapefruit, papaya, pomegranates, or mangoes until I went to California. Ethnic foods were generally not available. We sampled tacos first when Mary introduced them, having learned from her Tucson schoolmate at Moody. Having pizza was a big deal—so delicious but available only at the local tavern, causing some embarrassment in getting it. I tasted gefilte fish, pickled herring, and locks and bagels only much later in Connecticut. Much of our food, as might be expected, had German origins, such as the sauerkraut, occasional German potato salad, *mauldresher, fettdotchers*, apple *chalat,* and *kuchen*. Occasionally, though, we did have more exotic treats—for example, oyster soup (from canned oysters), special cheeses from Wisconsin, water cress salad (the cress sometimes found growing in the creek shallows), etc.

Except for family reunions (held at someone's house or in a public park), we almost never ate out. In fact, I can remember only once that our family ate out in a restaurant. On our way home from Freeport, as we were coming into Shannon, Dad said, "Let's eat here at this café," taking everyone by surprise. (I even remember what I had to eat on that occasion—a roast beef sandwich, open-faced, smothered with dark gravy. I thought we were really "up-town," even though the town had a population of only about 1100.)

The meals our family enjoyed together over the years were always special, though they seemed routine and mundane then. We always sat down together, around the oval wooden table covered with oilcloth, using chipped tin plates, saucers, and cups. There's something about sitting down and eating together that breaks down barriers and fosters good will. (It's instructive to note that the word *"companion"* is derived from the Latin words *"com"* plus *"panis"*—literally "with bread," "a bread-fellow," "those who eat bread together." We were not only brothers, sisters, and parents but also genuine "companions.") We said grace and we talked to each other, sometimes more than at other times. Certain rules applied, whether articulated or not. Everyone was expected to come promptly when the meal was announced (in earlier years with a bell in the Bell Tree being rung to summon the men from the fields). No shouting, loud speaking, quarreling, or crude behavior was permitted at the table. An unspoken stipulation was: "If you don't have anything good to say, it's best to keep quiet." We were expected to eat what was prepared—or go without. There was no catering to dislikes. We were also expected at least to *try* the food prepared, even if we didn't—or thought we didn't—like it. No one was to take more food than he/she could eat, and all food taken had to be eaten, including the fat on the meat, so nothing would be wasted (but we were never lectured about "starving children in China"). Finally, dessert was never permitted unless one had eaten some of the main course. Controversies over such matters as who would get to break the chicken wishbone or get the extra piece of pie were ordinarily settled justly and amicably.

Eating together, enjoying both the food and the camaraderie of family, is significant, so much so that Jesus Himself used it as a metaphor when He said, "Look at me. I stand at the door. I knock. If you hear me call and open the door, I'll come right in and sit down to supper with you" (Revelation 3:20, *The Message*). The Lord Jesus was the unseen, but no less real, guest through all those meals at that oval wooden table covered with oilcloth, with food on chipped enamel plates, with drink in "tumblers"— and, it is to be hoped, in each of our hearts. *Bon appetit.*

Appendix: Other Kehl Family Recipes

Panned Summer Squash
Prepare young, tender squash by cutting into small pieces. Leave skin on unless too tough. Melt a little butter in a skillet and brown slightly. Then dump in squash. Season. Cover and cook 10-15 minutes at a moderately

low heat. Remove the cover and cook a little longer so the liquid can evaporate. Serve hot.

Red Kidney Bean Salad
Pour water over 1 can beans. Drain and add:
3 hard-boiled eggs, diced
6 small sweet pickles, diced
1 onion cut in small pieces
½ to 1 stalk celery, diced
Serve with mayonnaise or the following:
½ cup vinegar
½ cup sugar
1 egg (well beaten)
½ teaspoon mustard
Cook until thickened.

Sliced Cucumber Pickles
Slice and let stand in heavy salt water a few hours.
1 gallon medium large cucumbers
3 onions
2 green and 1 red pepper
Drain. Make a syrup of:
3 cups vinegar
3 cups sugar
1 tablespoon mustard seed
1 tablespoon celery seed
When hot, add pickles and boil 5 minutes. Add dill as you fill the jars if you wish. Seal hot.

Apple Pickles
3½ cups sugar
3 cups vinegar
4 cups water
1 teaspoon stick cinnamon
¾ teaspoon salt
½ teaspoon whole cloves
Bring to boil. Add sweet apples and cover until soft. Can.

Tomato Catsup
1 gallon tomatoes (strained)
6 tablespoons salt
1½ tablespoons pepper
1 tablespoon cloves
2 tablespoons cinnamon
1 tablespoon allspice
1½ pint vinegar
1½ cups sugar
2 tablespoons dry mustard
Pinch of turmeric
1 teaspoon red pepper
Boil down about ½. (The tomatoes should be cooked, then strained to remove seeds and skins.)

Carrot Salad (Aunt Ella)
2 boxes of orange or lime jello
1½ cups graded carrots
1 can crushed pineapple
Marshmallows (optional)

Cranberry Salad (Aunt Lula)
1 pound cranberries, ground
1 cup apples
Ground rind and juice of 1 orange
2 cups sugar
Let stand overnight.
Add:
1 cup crushed pineapple
1 cup marshmallows, cut fine (optional)
1 cup nuts

Salad (Aunt Lula)
Marshmallows
1 cup pineapple chunks
1 cup grapes
1 cup (little) orange slices
1 cup sour cream

School Boy Favorites: Cookies
1/3 cup lard
1 cup brown sugar
1 egg
2 cups flour
½ teaspoon baking soda
½ teaspoon salt
1 teaspoon cinnamon
¼ teaspoon nutmeg
½ cup sour cream
1 cup chopped dates or raisins
Cream lard, sugar and egg until fluffy. Add sifted dry ingredients alternately with sour cream. Add dates or raisins. Drop by spoonfuls. Bake 10-12 minutes in a moderate 375 degree oven.

Cherry Crisp Pie (Aunt Lula)
Pour 1 can cherry pie filling in an 8 inch pie plate.
Put 1 cup white or yellow cake mix on the top.
Melt ½ stick butter or oleo over all. Bake at 400 degrees for 30 minutes. Top with whipped cream or Dream Whip.

Rhubarb Cream Pie (Aunt Lula)
Unbaked pie shell
3 cups rhubarb
1½ cups sugar
1 tablespoon butter
2 eggs, beaten
Mix together. Bake in 450 degree oven for 10 minutes, 350 degree for 30 minutes.

Sour Cream Chocolate Cake
Beat 1½ cups sour cream and 2 eggs together until thoroughly blended. Sift together:
1 cup sugar
1¾ cups flour
¼ teaspoon salt
1 teaspoon soda
5 pounds cocoa

On last sifting, add eggs and cream. Beat thoroughly. Add 1 teaspoon vanilla. Bake in greased pan in 325-degree oven for 20-25 minutes. Best to bake in loaf pan and frost with milk and sugar icing.

Milk and Sugar Icing
½ cup milk
1 cup sugar (Always ½ as much milk as sugar)
Boil until it forms a soft ball. Remove from heat and cool slightly. Heat until thick. Add 1 teaspoon vanilla. (If it gets too thick, add a few drops of milk.) (Mother used for cinnamon rolls.)

Fluffy White Icing
¾ cups sugar
¼ cup water
2 egg whites
1 teaspoon vanilla
Boil water and sugar until it spins an 8-inch thread (240-242 degrees). Keep pan covered for first 3 minutes. Beat egg whites. Pour hot syrup slowly into egg whites, heating constantly. Add vanilla. Continue heating until mixture is fluffy and will hold its shape.

Chocolate Pudding (Aunt Lula)
1 cup flour
2 teaspoons baking powder
½ teaspoon salt
¾ cup sugar
½ cup milk
2 tablespoons cocoa
1 teaspoon vanilla
2 tablespoons melted shortening
¾ cup chopped walnuts
1 cup brown sugar
¼ cup cocoa
1¾ cups hot water
Sift flour, baking powder, sugar, salt and cocoa. Add milk, vanilla, and shortening. Beat. Add nuts and flour into cake tin. Now mix brown sugar and cocoa. Sprinkle on top of batter. Pour hot water over. Bake at 350 degrees for 45 minutes.

Steamed Chocolate Pudding (Mary's specialty)
1 cup sifted flour
1½ teaspoon baking powder
1/8 teaspoon salt
2 tablespoons shortening
½ teaspoon vanilla
½ cup sugar
1 egg, beaten
2 squares unsweetened chocolate (melted)
½ cup milk
Sift flour, baking powder and salt. Cream shortening and sugar. Add vanilla and egg. Beat well. Add chocolate. Add dry ingredients to sugar mixture alternately with milk. Grease top of double boiler. Fill not more than 2/3 full. Cover tightly and place over rapidly boiling water. Steam 1-1 ½ hours or until firm on top. Serve hot with light cream or hard sauce.

Steamed Molasses Pudding
1 egg, beaten
1 cup molasses
½ cup cold water
1 cup flour
1 teaspoon soda
½ teaspoon salt
1 cup chopped nuts
Mix together egg, molasses, and water. Add dry ingredients. Steam pudding in a greased mold or 1 pound coffee can for 1 hour. Serve with sauce or whipped cream.

Hard Sauce
Cream 1/3 cup butter
Gradually add: 1 cup powdered sugar and 1 teaspoon vanilla or lemon flavoring. Cool and serve with steamed chocolate pudding.

VIII. A Legacy of Faith

"Faith of our fathers, holy faith,
We will be true to thee till death."
              (F. W. Faber, "Faith of Our Fathers")

"How blessed are the children
Who in their parents see
The tender Father-love of God,
And find their way to Thee."
          (Lois S. Johnson, "Our Thanks, O God, for Fathers")

"Happy the home where Jesus' name
Is sweet to every ear,
Where children early lisp His fame
And parents hold Him dear."
    (Henry Ware, "Happy the Home When God Is There")

"Now thank we all our God
With hearts and hands and voices … ,
Who from our mother's arms
Hath blessed us on our way
With countless gifts of love,
And still is ours today."
          (Martin Rinkart, "Now Thank We All Our God")

" In this faith I will to live and die."
             (Francois Villon, "Ballade de l'Homage")

"Our hearts, our hopes, our prayers, our tears,
Our faith triumphant o'er our fears,
Are all with thee—are all with thee."
                         (Henry Wadsworth Longfellow,
                              "The Building of the Ship")

"Now God be praised, that to believing souls
Gives light in darkness, comfort in despair."
                    (Shakespeare, *King Henry the Sixth*, Part II)

"Blessed are those who have not seen and yet believe."
                                        (Jesus, John 20:29)

In one of his psalms, Asaph, apparently during a time of great adversity, wrote, "I shall remember the deeds of the Lord; surely I will remember Thy wonders of old, I will meditate on all Thy work, and muse on Thy deeds" (Psalm 77:11-12). In a similar way, David, in Psalm 105, enumerates the various wonderful works of the Lord on behalf of Israel, and again, in Psalm 143, David writes, "I remember the days of old; I meditate on all Thy doings; I muse on the work of Thy hands" (5). When we, like the psalmists, wonder, "Has God forgotten to be gracious? Or has He in anger withdrawn His compassion?" (77:9), we can go back to our spiritual monuments that mark God's wondrous works on our behalf in the past. The express purpose of this chapter is to reflect on the wondrous works of God on behalf of our family.

A logical place for such a monument would be on the Kehl farm during the Depression days, a Sunday afternoon in the late 30s, probably 1938 or 1939, when our Mother tuned the Philco radio to WMBI, the Moody station from Chicago, and with her family listened to Charles E. Fuller's Old Fashioned Revival Hour originating in Long Beach, California. The family heard the quartet, with the masterful piano accompaniment of Rudy Atwood, the singing of "Heavenly Sunshine," the reading of letters by Mrs. Fuller ("Go right ahead, honey"), and a brief message from the Word of God, concluded with an invitation to receive Jesus Christ as personal Savior. On that occasion, Mother asked the family to bow with her and pray for salvation. I was too young to participate, but I have heard that each member of the family did, in fact, bow with Mother that day and pray to receive Christ as Savior! What a monument to polish and ponder!

Thankfully, that blessed occasion, however, was neither the first nor the last dealing that God had with the Kehl family. In fact, the Apostle Paul tells us in Ephesians 1 that "He chose us in Him before the foundation of the world, that we should be holy and blameless before Him. In love He predestined us to adoption as children through Jesus Christ to Himself, according to the kind intention of His will, to the praise of the glory of His grace, which He freely bestowed on us in the Beloved" (4-6). He chose the Kehl family even before He laid the foundations of the world—and ordained that Sunday afternoon when the family put their faith in Him, for if He had not drawn them, they would not, could not, have come (John 6:44, 65). He "ordained the days for us, when as yet there was not one of them"; He formed our inward parts and wove us in our mother's womb (Psalm 139:16, 13). And "before He formed us in the womb He knew us, and before we were born He consecrated us" (Jeremiah 1:5). We offer grateful thanks to Him, for we are indeed "fearfully and wonderfully made. Wonderful are His works!" (Psalm 139:14).

It's interesting to trace the Lord's leading in the lives of the Kehl family. As noted in Chapter II, our mother, Anna Carrie Albrecht, was brought up in the German Lutheran tradition, attended German Lutheran school for catechism, and was confirmed. Even then, when she was a young girl, God's Holy Spirit was apparently speaking to her, but she told us later that she never once heard about the necessity of being born again and having a personal relationship with the Lord Jesus. After she married our father, Harry William Kehl, on November 29, 1923, it was apparently a foregone conclusion that they would attend the Methodist Episcopal church in Mt. Carroll, the church of his family, and that is where all of the Kehl children were sprinkled. My own birth certificate, dated the 3rd day of October, 1937, and signed by Pastor G. P. Nesmith, quotes eight passages of Scripture, including Matthew 18:14 ("Even so it is not the will of your Father which is in heaven that one of these little ones should perish") and Mark 10:14 ("Suffer the little children to come unto me, and forbid them not; for of such is the kingdom of God"). In addition, it includes several prayers of dedication: "O Son, who diedst for us, behold / We bring our child to Thee! / Great Shepherd, take it to Thy fold, / Thine own for aye to be: / Defend it through this earthly strife, / And lead it on the path of life." And this one: "This child we dedicate to Thee / O God of grace and purity! / Shield it from sin and threatening wrong / And let Thy love its life prolong." Those are good prayers of dedication. In smaller print, the certificate states: "Baptism is not merely a token of the Christian profession, whereby Christians are distinguished from others and whereby they obligate themselves to observe every Christian duty, but it is also a sign of internal ablution, or the new birth." The "obligation," I assume, was intended for my parents, and my mother especially took seriously the obligation to observe every Christian duty, specifically to bring me up in the nurture and admonition of the Lord. But how could there be "internal ablution, or new birth" at this point, because I was only one year and 21 days old? The new birth was to come about four years later, when I could understand and exercise my will. (According to family lore, during one Sunday morning service I, as a toddler, made my way toward the pastor at the front, almost reaching the chancel before my embarrassed father could catch and retrieve me.)

Mother was faithful in getting six kids up, fed breakfast, bathed, and dressed (as we were in the accompanying snapshot, standing in stair-step order in the yard one Sunday morning, none of us much liking it but doing it dutifully at Mother's insistence), before driving off in the Model-A the seven miles to town (with Mother invariably wetting the corner of her handkerchief to remove a last, missed, or newly-acquired smudge or to smooth down a recalcitrant cowlick), each of us with dimes and nickels (egg money) tied in handkerchiefs for Sunday School offerings.

We always felt conspicuous and out-of-place as country kids among all the town kids—and especially in a congregation that included the prominent town banker, insurance salesman, and various merchants, all impeccably dressed, with their families, walking to church from their upscale town homes or driving expensive new automobiles. It was a so-called "social gospel" we heard proclaimed: be honest, be kind, "live and let live." One sermon consisted of a story entitled "Little Boy Blue." Another Sunday morning that made a big impression was a talk by one of the seven companions of Capt. Eddie Rickenbacker, the eight having been forced down in the Pacific in 1942, about 600 miles north of Samoa and who were rescued after drifting 24 days on rubber rafts, the speaker duly acknowledging the hand of God in his survival and rescue.

God used the Sunday School and some of its dedicated teachers, such as Miss Jane DeNier (her "untimely" death at age 20 mentioned in Chapter III) and Mrs. Winsel McGrath, faithful wife of the rural mail carrier, who made a special effort to welcome the shy, retiring country kids and save each a Christmas sack (with hard candy, nuts, and a rare Florida orange—all a welcome treat) if we missed the Christmas Sunday festivities, which we often did because of inclement weather. (I wish I could express to her how much that meant to a shy, self-conscious country kid!) We were taught the Bible stories, and I still have a box of Sunday School papers and cards we received—some 60 Beginners Golden Text Cards (with pictures to color) and Beginners Lesson Pictures (from David C. Cook, Standard Publishing House, and Methodist Publishers), the dates ranging from 1940 to 1945. Also included are nearly 60 four-page Primary Class sheets with brightly colored pictures of Bible scenes, many of which resonate for me today (such as "David Cares for the Sheep," "Wise Men follow the Star," "Jesus Teaching from a Boat"). The oldest, titled "The Primary Quarterly," dated November 3, 1940, with my name scrawled on the front, has a picture of Jesus welcoming seven little children and the caption "Let the Children Come to Me." It also includes a story titled "Friendliness to Younger Children," based on Mark 10:13-16, along with a brief story called "A Traveling Home" along with a Farm Security Administration photograph by Dorothea Lange, depicting a migrant family headed west, crammed into a dilapidated old car with their possessions stacked on the running boards and tied on the sides. The story concludes, "What do they need that you can help to give them? Will you try to find out?" (At four years old, I'm afraid I didn't try to find out, but years later I was to research the influence of Lange and the FSA photographs on John Steinbeck's *The Grapes of Wrath*.) During those days, it was still customary for pastors to make a call on all members of the congregation at least once a year. The Rev. Frank Countryman called at the farm at least once, but was averse to going out into the field to talk to the men or to stay for a meal.

During those tender years, I treasured such books as *The Life of Christ Visualized*, (Standard Publishing Company, 1942-1943), *Bible Stories* (with pictures to color or paint) (Whitman Publishing Company, Racine, Wisconsin, 1939), and others. Also dated 1940 are the Central Press Association's "Illustrated Sunday School Lessons" (in cartoon form with Scripture citations beneath) that appeared in *The Clinton Herald*, the newspaper which our family received by mail (a day late), and which I cut out and pasted in scrapbooks. On a sheet of paper, dated 1941, I wrote: "I tuch Jesus as my persnl savyur" and "I deasided I am going to be a minister." If I recall correctly, Aunt Ida gave me my first Bible and my parents gave me a little black New Testament when I was 9. I recall how thrilled I was to receive a New Testament when the Gideons came to Sage School (and still have that well-worn 1943 edition and a 1946 Army edition). Another booklet I made includes prayers that service men would come back safely and that the war would end soon (signed Rev. Delmar G. Kehl, U. S. Marine Corps).

When asked what I'd like for a Christmas or birthday gift, I ordinarily requested "a Jesus book." I received books of Christian fiction (such as *Winkie Lost in the Rockies, Thine Is the Kingdom*, and others), and still have a book I received from my brother Maynard for Christmas of 1951, Harry J. Albus' *A Treasury of Dwight L. Moody* (Eerdmans, 1949) and *The Life of Dwight L. Moody* by his son (Revell, 1900), which my brother found for me at a family auction.

The Philco radio played a further role in the Christian growth of the family. Working around the house—cooking, baking, cleaning, sewing, wallpapering—my mother listened to Christian programs. Regulars on WMBI were the noon Hymn Sing from Crowell Hall at Moody (and later, on one occasion, Mother, my sisters, and I were there in person), "The Story" (a daily dramatization of Bible stories), the weekly (Saturday evenings) broadcast of Pacific Garden Mission's "Unshackled" (dramatizations of stories about transformed lives at the Mission), as well as Fuller's "Old Fashioned Revival Hour," M. R. DeHaan's "Radio Bible Class" (from Grand Rapids, Michigan), Theodore Epp's "Back to the Bible Broadcast" (from Lincoln, Nebraska), William Pettingill's broadcast (Waterloo, Iowa), E. Howard Cadle's broadcast, William Ward Ayer's broadcast, and, of course, Billy Graham's "Hour of Decision." In the summer there were the broadcasts from Winona Lake Bible Conference, with such speakers as William Culbertson, M. R. DeHaan, Walter L. Wilson, James McGinley, Bob Jones Sr. and Jr., John R. Rice, Clifford Lewis, Monroe Parker, J. Palmer Muntz, William Ward Ayer, Stephen Olford, and others. I was captivated by these messages and would often take notes and discuss them with Mother. She sent for various books and subscribed to *The Sword of the Lord*, which she read faithfully every Sunday afternoon and evening, along with her large, well-worn Bible.

On Saturdays my sisters and I would listen to the KYB club (I recently ran across a blue and white KYB Club / WMBI pin) and Children's Bible Hour (with Mel Johnson). (I also found a small CBH pin, with gold lettering on red background, with an open Bible, a microphone, and the time of the program: 10:00 A. M. Saturday.) (I also found a receipt from "The Children's Bible Hour," dated April 12, 1944, thanking me for my gift of .25: "This gift is gratefully received and will help many others to hear about Jesus!"). Mother also encouraged me to sign up with the Bible Memory Association to learn assigned verses each week, recite them to someone (other than a parent or family member; Mrs. Katzenberger, a dear saint, graciously listened to mine), and receive Christian books and other prizes.

Mother didn't leave Christian instruction to church, Sunday school, and books. She and Dad taught us moral values, both by verbal instruction and, even more importantly, by example. They had a reputation in the community for integrity, for being inveterately honest, paying their bills in full and on time, in cash. They were true to their word; if they said they would do something, you could count on its being done. They were both hard workers, doing their very best in everything they set about doing. Mother often reminded us that "you don't get something for nothing," that the world didn't owe us a living. The word and concept of "entitlement" were foreign to us. She always told us kids that in school the grades we received were less important than doing our very best. We were always taught to finish the job we started and not to put off doing what needed to be done. Our parents worked hard on six days, but they considered Sunday a day of rest, with only necessary work being done. Dad often fretted over neighbors who worked on Sunday, insisting that he could get more done in six days than they in seven. Further, our parents neither used nor permitted profanity or obscenity. As noted earlier, once when I used a profane word I had heard at school, the look I received from Mother was enough to convince me never to use it again—and I didn't. Expressions such as "man," "man-o-man," "boy," "boy-o-boy" were less offensive, apparently because it was thought that an expletive that takes man's name in vain is preferable to one that takes God's name in vain. Also a bit less reprehensible were scatological expressions, although Mother frowned upon them and was never heard to use them herself. (See more in "Kehl Talk," Chapter V.)

Dad never drank alcoholic beverages and smoked only an occasional cigar, though he chewed tobacco (a habit started, he said, during long days working in the hot sun). Both Mother and Dad were also quite generous, altruistic, often giving produce (for example, tomatoes, watermelons, strawberries, apples, grapes) to neighbors and friends. Dad was generous also in helping neighbors when they had a special need, either to assist in harvesting crops or to help fix a mechanical problem, and when he was owed something, he never pressed for payment, never collected bills (as Mother didn't when her own brothers owed her money, which was sorely needed during the Depression years). Mother made a special effort to treat each of her children equitably, while, of course, being sensitive to our different needs. She often admonished us never to quarrel over material things or let them become a divisive element disrupting our relationships: "Don't you kids fight over things when we're gone!"—and we never did. Mother and Dad were eminently practical, pragmatic—though they knew nothing of William James' treatises on pragmatism: "The pragmatic method traces practical consequences. What difference would it practically make to any one if this notion rather than that notion were true? If no practical difference whatever can be traced, then the alternatives mean practically the same thing, and all dispute is idle ... The pragmatist turns away from abstraction and insufficiency, from verbal solutions ... He turns towards concreteness and adequacy, towards facts, towards action." But as a believer, Mother turned first to the Scripture and prayer to seek God's will in determining a course of action or in making an ethical decision.

Another key value Mother taught us both by example and by instruction had to do with worry. I recall how Mother often worried about a variety of issues: about whether there would be enough money to pay the bills and buy necessities, about raising six children in the Christian faith, about the safety and welfare of the family, particularly when Dad or my brothers were late in getting home on a stormy day, about tornadoes and thunderstorms and lightning, about one of the chimneys "burning out" (fire going up the chimney with the danger of catching the house on fire), etc. And then one day, from reading Christian literature ("God's Cure for Anxious Care"), she announced her life-changing insight, surely something of an epiphany: "When you're worrying, you're not trusting the Lord—and it's a sin to worry. God tells us to 'be anxious for *nothing*, but in *everything* by prayer and supplication with thanksgiving, let your requests be made known unto God'" (Philippians 4:6). From that day, by an act of her will and trust in God's care, she demonstrated the peace of God that surpasses all understanding, and she set an example for us all.

Mother's listening to Christian radio programs and reading Christian books and periodicals soon revealed to her that the gospel news of salvation was not being proclaimed in the church we were attending. One of the main sponsors of county-wide "revival" meetings at the local high school auditorium was the Church of God (headquarters in Harrisburg, PA), so we started attending there. The pastor was the Rev. Carl V. Binkley, who subsequently baptized us by immersion on May 21, 1950, in the muddy Plum River in Pleasant Valley (Mother was baptized later), and welcomed us into membership. Maynard and family began attending the Church of God after the birth of their first daughter, Barbara, and they joined the church on May 14, 1950. Pastor Binkley invited them to church while he was doing some wiring at their home (when the electricity came through in 1949). John and his family were also long-time members of the church and were very active, serving on boards and committees, and teaching Sunday School.

One series of revival meetings were led by Evangelist James V. Lamb, who demonstrated zeal in going out into the countryside and speaking to individuals about their personal salvation. I caught some of the zeal and took fliers and tracts to neighbors, inviting them to come, including the Tiptons, Judases, and Nowaks (and used "The Wordless Book" and prayed with Bob and Lloyd to receive Christ as Savior). Another series of meetings were led by Evangelist Bill Rice, with the singing led by Straton Shufelt. The first night I volunteered to sing in the choir—but to my disappointment was told that I was too young, that this was an adult choir. (I remember that my dad was demonstrably upset, something rare for him, and he went to speak with the evangelist on my behalf, but I made the decision to honor their stipulation and not sing.)

Berreman Church of God

Other special meetings were held at the Pleasant Valley Church of God, with Rev. Nick Anderson preaching one year and Rev. Wesley Fornwalt another. Special meetings were held in Freeport, with Rev. Hyman Appelman (a converted Jew) preaching (we attended on a Sunday afternoon, joining an overflow crowd), and tent meetings were held in Clinton, Iowa, with Rev. Clifford Lewis speaking. John and I went to those meetings on his Harley-Davidson, and on the first night, at the singing of "Where He Leads Me I Will Follow," I went forward to surrender my life to His service. (John and I met a really cute girl who sang in the choir, but nothing came of it.)

I also attended summer camp at Camp Berreman, at Berreman Church of God, a little country church about five miles from the family farm. This was before dormitories were built, so we slept in tents pitched in a pasture adjacent to the church. We had classes all morning, recreation in the afternoon, and preaching services at night. The preacher was Rev. John D. English, with music led by Rev. Cyrus Pollard, pastor of the church. Rev. Mr. English was an effective communicator (and I remember asking for his notes). The class I took, on basic Christian beliefs, was taught by Rev. Nick

Anderson. One morning he called on me to lead in prayer, thinking I had prayed in public before—but I hadn't, and I was flummoxed. He apologized later and offered helpful encouragement. When I raised questions about the church's Arminian beliefs concerning the security of the believer, he suggested I talk further to my pastor. Questions: "If I receive 'eternal' life and it ends, it wasn't 'eternal,' was it?" "If I am born again as a child of God, how can I be 'unborn'"? "Didn't Jesus say that no one can pluck us out of the Father's hand? Can we be any more secure than that?" Answer: "Oh, it's true that no one can pluck us out of the Father's hand, but we can jump out." "Oh."

I struggled with the security issue for years, even, in some desperation, writing to prominent Christian leaders (Charles E. Fuller, Bob Jones, John R. Rice, Billy Graham), asking for clarification. At the same time, I began to doubt my salvation, thinking that if I didn't *feel* a certain way or didn't *feel* saved, then I must not be. Several passages of Scripture especially disturbed me—for example, I John 5:18 ("We know that whosoever is born of God sinneth not"). Hebrews 10:26 struck terror to my heart: "If we sin willfully after we have received the knowledge of the truth, there remaineth no more sacrifice for sins, But a certain fearful looking for of judgment and fiery indignation." Had I sinned willfully? Yes, haven't we all, numbers of times? Did this mean I was eternally lost, beyond redemption? Hebrews 6:4-6 also caused deep concern, seeming to say that after having tasted the good word and even having been a partaker of the Holy Spirit, if such a one "falls away," it is impossible to renew that one to repentance because they "crucify to themselves the Son of God afresh and put him to an open shame." I tried to reason with myself as follows: "Scripture says that 'whoever will call upon the name of the Lord will be saved' (Romans 10:13). Have you called on the name of the Lord? Yes, the best I know how. Then you must be saved." Assurance would last until my next slip-up, then doubts would come again. Maybe I hadn't adequately repented …

Around this time, I saw the title of a sermon in a Christian paper—"The Unpardonable Sin," a sin so heinous, so egregious, that it can never be forgiven. I couldn't bring myself to read the sermon, because I knew I must have committed this sin. I remember vividly that Sunday afternoon. My parents were taking a nap (I never could understand why adults would want to waste valuable time sleeping when there were so many things to do or get into), my brothers were off somewhere, my sisters were preoccupied elsewhere. I can't describe the terror I felt as I walked out to the barn and around the barnyard—sheer, abject terror of being lost forever, separated eternally from God, in outer darkness. Should I talk to my older sister? Surely my mom would have given wise counsel. I mustered courage to read the sermon and learned that the unpardonable sin is blasphemy against the Holy Spirit and fear that one has committed it is probably an indication that such is not the case, for one who has committed it is beyond feeling.

Another stage of this spiritual struggle had to do with the second coming of Christ, the secret rapture of the church. I recall coming home from school one afternoon and, not finding anyone in the house, I began to panic, thinking all the family had been taken to heaven and I had been left behind. What a relief it was to find them all out in the garden digging potatoes! Never had digging potatoes seemed so special!

Knowing that I had expressed the intention of becoming a minister, Pastor Binkley, who tooled around in a Nash Rambler, arranged for me to "preach" on a Sunday evening (when I was about eleven or twelve). One of the early "messages" was on Psalm 92:12-13—"The righteous shall flourish like the palm tree; he shall grow like a cedar in Lebanon. Those who are planted in the house of the Lord shall flourish in the courts of our God." Of course, at that time I had never so much as seen a palm tree or a cedar, for that matter, but I made connections to "the tree planted by the rivers of water, that brings forth its fruit in its season; its leaf also shall not wither; and whatever he does shall prosper" (Psalm 1:3). Pastor Binkley made helpful notes critiquing the content and delivery: "Begin without apologizing [for being young and inexperienced], emphasize positive points from the Scripture. Next time why don't you speak on a topic like faith?" "But what does a young kid like me know about faith that would be beneficial to share with these people?"—those were my thoughts as I drove the tractor raking hay and baling hay. Somehow I made it through, with help from Mother's Christian literature. (Edna Weber, a spinster lady, said after one message, "You did a good job, but I remember reading that in *The Sword of the Lord*.")

When we moved from the farm to town in January of 1953, we were able to walk to church twice on Sundays and for the midweek prayer service. Even when Dad sometimes said he was too tired to go and we kids didn't always feel so inclined, Mother would say, "Let's go, kids. We don't want to be late." When I left for college in September of 1953, Pastor Binkley came by the house to pray with us and wish us Godspeed. When I was in college, Mother faithfully wrote a letter each Sunday afternoon, relating the news and assuring me of her prayers, a letter which I could regularly expect to receive each Wednesday. (When she heard that I was corresponding with a local Catholic girl, she wrote a long letter expressing her concern ["That really bothers my brains!"] about believers being "unequally yoked together with unbelievers," an rebuke that I sorely needed.)

In his novel *Godric*, Frederick Buechner writes, "When a man leaves home, he leaves behind some scrap of his heart." That was so when I left home at sixteen—and I'm sure it was true as well for my sisters and oldest brother, when he left for the Navy. But we also sent "a scrap of [our] heart ahead," as Buechner adds, due in large part to our mother's strong Christian faith that influenced us all, even to this day. One example of that pervasive influence occurred after I had completed a year of graduate study at the University of Wisconsin and was negotiating for a teaching job at a prep school in Stamford, Connecticut. The year was 1958, but in that small town telephones were still "party lines," which meant that we shared the line with others on the block. I dialed the number and then heard a click, which was Mrs. McCray across the street, who minded everyone's business, listening in to determine if that Kehl boy was going to get a job or if he was planning to go to school all his life! I'm afraid I lost my cool and said, "Listen, you old biddy! Why don't you mind your own business? Get off the line!" The phone clicked, I made my call to Connecticut, and hung up after being assured that I had the job. But the rejoicing was short-lived, because there was Mother's reproachful look: she had a Christian testimony to maintain among the neighbors, who saw her leave for church each week. No words were necessary. I knew what I had to do. After several hours of pure misery, I made my way across the street—and apologized to Mrs. McCray, telling her that as a Christian I was asking her to forgive my rudeness. After some stern looks and sounds ("Humph"), she accepted my apology and became a good friend, who always greeted me when I came back home on subsequent occasions.

Mother was to die of cancer just a year and a half later, and Dad lived twenty-one years after that. Mother was never to meet Wanda, our two sons, Kevin and Kenyon, our daughters-in-law, Kathie and Josette, or our five grandchildren, Emily, Aidan, Owen, Bennett, and Brynn, but I believe she knows of them. According to the voice the Apostle John heard from heaven, "Blessed are the dead who die in the Lord ... that they may rest from their labors, and their works do follow them" (Revelation 14:13).

The spiritual legacy lives on. We treasure this monument of God's abundant grace, this legacy of faith.

Conclusion:
A Good Beginning and a Good End

"Begin at the beginning … and go on till you come to the end: then stop."
(Lewis Carroll, *Alice's Adventures in Wonderland)*

"The fairest things have fleetest end,
Their scent survives their close."
(Francis Thompson, "Daisy")

"Of a good beginning cometh a good end."
(John Heywood, *Proverbs)*

"The end crowns all."   (Shakespeare, *Troilus and Cressida)*

"So we see some chapters of our lives come to their natural end."
(Sarah Orne Jewett, *The Country of the Pointed Firs)*

"Life is the art of drawing sufficient conclusions from insufficient premises."   (Samuel Butler, *Notebooks)*

"Not to conclude against a wall of stone."
(Richard Wilbur, "Mind")

One of the proverbs of the 17th century writer John Heywood says, "Of a good beginning comes a good end." As this discourse has shown, the Kehl family had a good beginning, with the six siblings having a godly, nurturing mother and an upright, hard-working father who provided well for us and gave us a good start. Our Lord, Who is both "the beginning and the end," Who sees the start and the finish, has blessed us with His abundant grace through the years.

Life itself, Samuel Butler wrote in his *Notebook*, is "the art of drawing sufficient conclusions from insufficient premises." The conclusions drawn here have, we hope, been sufficient, though they are necessarily drawn from insufficient, because incomplete and subjective, evidence and premises. Each of us remembers events, occurrences, and actions differently because Mnemosyne, the goddess of memory, is fickle and often fails us. But one conclusion we can draw with great authority—that which Qoheleth drew thousands of years ago: "Let us hear the conclusion of the whole matter: Fear God and keep His commandments, for this is the whole duty of man" (Ecclesiastes 12:13). This conclusion is strikingly similar to that of the prophet Micah: "He has told you, O man, what is good; And what does the Lord require of you but to do justice, to love kindness, and to walk humbly with your God?" (6:8), which, in turn, echoes the words of Moses in Deuteronomy: "What does the Lord your God require from you, but to fear the Lord your God, to walk in all His ways and love Him, and to serve the Lord your God with all your heart and with all your soul, and to keep the Lord's commandments and His statutes" (10: 12-13). We were taught to do the whole duty of man—fear God, keep His commandments, be just, be kind, walk humbly (carefully) in His ways, and love Him with all our soul. May this be the distinctive Kehl trademark, evidenced in each individual family and in every member.

As we look back over the family's years of grace and God's rich blessings to us, we each should offer praise and thanksgiving to God for His mercy and lovingkindness. In the Introduction we began by specifying eight functions which a family accomplishes in the lives of its members. Here, after having examined the sense of place, the sense of family roots, shared memories, family expressions, school experiences, food and eating, and our legacy of faith, we can specify five other effects which the family had on each of us.

First, the Kehl family provided each of us with a strong sense of identity, of identification, of who we were: We are Kehls—and proud of it! I recall hearing comments like this: "Oh, you must be Harry Kehl's boy.

I've known Harry for years. Has a farm northa Carroll. Good man. Honest as the day is long." Or: "Oh, are you Mel's (or Maynard's or John's) brother? Helped me get my car started one time. Pulled me outa' the ditch another time." Kehl was a name to be proud of, to cherish, to honor and not bring reproach on it. In a similar way, as members of the family of God, we are admonished to "walk in a manner worthy of the God who calls [us] into His own kingdom and glory" (I Thessalonians 2:12), to "walk in a manner worthy of the calling with which [we] have been called" (Ephesians 4:1).

The family also aided us in establishing ongoing relationships that required getting along, a give- and-take, learning to compromise. Learning to live amicably with five siblings in all kinds of situations and circumstances taught us about fellowship (*koinonia*), sharing, having things in common yet learning to be unique individuals with diversified interests, desires, and needs. Family life serves to take off some of the rough edges and help members learn to get along, a lesson valuable later in community, both secular society and the community of believers.

Family life also taught us about authority and respect. Because we learned respect for and obedience to the authority of our parents, we readily came to recognize the authority of God our Heavenly Father, Who is worthy of our obedience and reverential awe. We learned about and saw evidence of "tough love" when our parents had to discipline us for wrongdoings, just as we receive divine discipline, "for those whom the Lord loves He disciplines, and He chastens those He accepts as His children" (Hebrews 12:6).

Another key function of the family was to teach right and wrong and help us make positive ethical decisions. We all remember the strong moral code modeled and established by our parents, so authoritative that Mother could convey her expectations with a look and Dad could say forthrightly, "You don't want to do that!" The value formation discussed in Chapter VIII is a major part of our priceless spiritual legacy.

Finally, the family provided a secure sanctuary, a place of refuge in which to find acceptance, solace, and encouragement after the relentless assaults at school or work. It was a place to be built up, fortified, strengthened after being torn down, demoralized, and weakened by a world that is no friend of grace. The family was a place, a condition, of grace—filial favor unmerited, unearned, and unending.

Much more could be said of the Kehls. I wish there were more material and stories about each of us (but especially about and from Mel, John, and Carolyn). There could be further chapters about the lives and work of each sibling after we left the nest, our children, our grandchildren. But those other chapters need to be written by each of those who know them best. This is just a beginning—but of a good beginning comes a good end, shaped by a legacy of faith and years of grace—and grit. May we all end well.